RMS Carpathia
Triumph and Tragedy of the Titanic Rescue Ship

William Baird

Copyright © 2017 William Baird

All rights reserved.

ISBN: 154558589X
ISBN-13: 9781545585894

DEDICATION

To my family as always.

I would also like to dedicate this book to those incredible people who surface and thrive in the most trying and consequential moments when people's lives are in danger. In this book that person is Arthur H. Rostron; Captain of the RMS *Carpathia*. In contemporary times, Airline Pilot Chesley Sullenberger is our example. In both cases, on-the-spot critical decisions and the actions ensuing from those decisions saved many lives. However, lives in the balance cannot be saved in a moment as they both faced without all those who play anonymous roles; crew members, physicians, brave survivors, and what today we call First Responders. Life and death decisions can be made but require the incredible talents and dedication of those who act on those decisions to save their fellow human beings.

I dedicate this book to those people.

William Baird

2017

ACKNOWLEDGMENTS

As always, no researcher or author can complete any project without librarians all over the world who are always so eager to assist. They are the unsung heroes. Special thanks go to the efficient people at the U.K. National Archives, John Winrow at the Maritime Archives, the Liverpool Museums, and librarians in Easthampton and Montauk, N.Y., among others, who answered innumerable questions fully and cheerfully. I am very appreciative of some of the authors of the books listed as sources who freely shared their knowledge by phone and email. A special mention needs to be made to the stunning amount of information already compiled by Encyclopedia Titanica. U-Boat.net and Wikipedia were very useful for specific and general research. Heather Baird, Rick Meeks, and Rick Smith were again so valuable in listening to me bounce half-formed ideas off of them and in helping to edit my project.

CONTENTS

Acknowledgments

1. The Friendly Ship — 1
2. Fateful Journey — 24
3. Calling for Help — 51
4. Consequential Acts — 74
5. Refuge and Regret — 92
6. Final Destination — 119
7. Appreciation and Recrimination — 140
8. The Gathering Storm — 161
9. World at War — 185
10. Death of a Lady — 200

Afterword — 213

Sources — 218

TO THE READER

When I arbitrarily selected the RMS *Carpathia* for the voyage of one of my family characters in my book *Unexpected Journeys*, I had no idea of the short and fascinating story of the Cunard liner. She was just a name to me. As I researched her compelling history, I realized that her story had seldom been told. I also realized that the ship itself should be the main character of this saga, but the story needed to be told through the two main human characters on her most famous voyage in 1912: Arthur Rostron, the captain of the *Carpathia*, and Marconi operator Harold Cottam. While, for storytelling purposes, I have adjusted Cottam's pre and post 1912 history, and the relationship with Elizabeth Hadnot, his words and actions during the *Titanic* disaster are based on actual statements and interviews. I have supplied a full summary of Cottam's career and life in the afterword. The same standard is true for the remarkable Arthur Rostron. His words and actions are well documented through his words and testimony, including a very unusual encounter at sea during his career. Elizabeth Hadnot, and her parents, are fictional characters based on an amalgam of actual *Titanic* passengers and their experiences.

On matters relating to the *Titanic*, I have striven to make this a contemporaneous account. Of the multiple theories and conclusions as to the sinking and the actions of the people involved, I have tried not to embrace one over another. The various theories and differing accounts are treated as conversations, impressions, and gossip of the day. They are based on witness statements and the investigations after the sinking, plus current research. I will leave it to the reader to investigate and decide which they feel is the one "real" reason the *Titanic* ended up on the bottom of the Atlantic. The texts of the

Marconigrams are verbatim although in some cases, two messages are combined into one. The wartime actions of *Carpathia* are a blend of some of Rostron's wartime voyages in different ships and the limited actual historical information existing on *Carpathia*'s wartime experiences. The details of her final convoy and sinking are accurate and were surprisingly difficult to research.

I have consciously kept the seafaring and wireless radio jargon to a minimum. I did have to make my own decision on whether to call Harold's listening devices earphones, headphones, or telephones – all of which are used in various research sources.

I have included in an afterword what actually happened to some of the main historical characters and ships on which this book is based. One of the many ironies in this saga is that while a majority of combatant ships during WW1 survived the conflict, most of the great passenger liners of the era were casualties of war and ended up on the bottom of the sea.

I hope you enjoy learning about the gallant lady named RMS *Carpathia*.

William Baird

2017/2021

Chapter One

THE FRIENDLY SHIP

No one ever said she was beautiful. Or even pretty. Even as she aged, she never caught up to others considered prettier, quicker, more up to the minute, or more pleasing to the eye. She was thought of as comfortable and often mentioned as friendly. Dependable and steady were the labels assigned to her. No, things would never fall into place, as they say, for her to become a beauty. She would seek her worth and value in having a big heart. Those who came in contact with her would be treated with caring and concern for their well-being. Everyone would receive a compassionate touch, even those who society labeled as the lower classes. Her virtue would be found, not in physical attraction, but in being a haven for all and a promise of hope for the future.

Dressed all in red, black, and white and with the promise of fascinating stops in exciting and exotic lands, she starts her journey. Her whole being seems to vibrate with excitement for the adventure ahead as she turns towards far distant horizons. Gibraltar, Malta, Algiers, Alexandria, Trieste, Fiume, Naples; warm sunshine and new experiences are ahead for her. New cultures and foods will go along with the warm breezes and sunshine as she leaves old Blighty behind.

She was born in England. Newcastle upon Tyne to be exact in northeast England where it rains at least one week out of every month, and the cool damp is an ever-present part of life. She was closer to Edinburgh, Scotland than to London. But she is all British.

Now the water along the dock churns under her, bringing up the smells of harbor water; decaying wood, tidal flats, and the other unidentifiable miasma of smells found in every port. She exhales a huge gust of smoke and her 9,000 horsepower roil the water under her black hull. The freshly painted red funnel shines in the unusual sunshine as the RMS *Carpathia*, of the Cunard Line, stands out to sea.

She is 558 feet long and 64 feet 6 inches wide; the largest Cunarder built up to the time she was launched under Captain Barr in 1903. Workers from Swan-Hunter & Wigham Richardson were still swarming over her when she slid from the slipways into the water for the first time. Since then, she has made her way from Liverpool to America and then been reassigned to the Mediterranean service. She is different from the flyers being built both then and now in 1909. The *Mauretania*, her fellow Swan-Hunter product has captured the Blue Riband just this September. The award for the fastest crossing of the Atlantic is cherished by its winners as a show of the prestige of the Cunard Line and their own ship. The *Carpathia* is different. Very different. She plies her trade carrying immigrants and cargo at a more stately speed. Her seven boilers drive her twin propellers to achieve a maximum speed of 14 knots. Her four masts are designed for the efficient and fast loading and unloading of cargo like lumber, wheat, cotton, and pig iron to and from her vast holds. She also carries the mail and takes on the proud designation as Royal Mail Ship as part of her identity.

Swan-Hunter has designed her for the immigrant trade that was exploding when she was launched and has shown no signs of slowing down. In 1904 alone, five to ten thousand immigrants were arriving in New York City every day. New York City had turned into the third-largest Hungarian city in the world and *Carpathia* was designed and built to take advantage of that market. With a special arrangement made between Cunard and the Hungarian government, she will carry tens of thousands of Hungarian immigrants along with thousands of Italian immigrants to the new world. But, unlike many other ships, she prides herself on carrying them in comfort. Third-class passengers will not be buried deep in the bowels of the ship. They are not sentenced to the thunder of her engines at the stern or the crash of the waves at the bow. The ship has been designed for nothing but second and third-class passengers and they will be housed on the upper decks. She didn't even have a first-class designation until a refit in 1905 to add cabins for 150 first-class passengers in an attempt to attract some of the new-style leisure voyage passengers traveling just for pleasure. Those second and third-class passengers will be pampered for one of the first times in the steamship era. Separate smoking rooms, cabins with both electric lights and oil lamps as a backup, fine wood accents, and spacious dining rooms are unlike anything seen before. As a Cunard pamphlet bragged:

The Cunarder Carpathia is one of the most popular steamers employed in the Atlantic passenger traffic. In addition to her special design, she is fitted with bilge keels which minimize rolling, watertight doors and bulkheads. The experience of those who have traveled on the Carpathia say she is one of the steadiest of Atlantic liners. She carries a complete installation of Marconi Wireless Apparatus.

Her passenger quarters are roomy and comfortable, and what is equally important, thoroughly ventilated. The spacious promenades not only allow for healthy perambulation but are also available for the usual deck games played on shipboard.

As in all Cunard steamers, special attention has been given to the catering arrangements, and the service and cuisine are up to the usual high standard of efficiency. No pains are spared to provide attractive menus, which appeal to the most fastidious.

From the first design of the General Arrangement Plans for the ship to the execution in fine woods, tiles, and finishes, to the detail and luxury of the entrances, berths, and dining, and public rooms, this is a ship apart from anything currently on the seas. She boasts a compliment of three doctors; one Hungarian, one Italian, and one English to care for the nationalities she carries. The same is true for the food served as it is tailored to the tastes of passengers from different countries.

Perhaps the *Liverpool Journal of Commerce* explained best how far from the previous normal the *Carpathia* is:

> *The captain's room and the chart room are located on the promenade deck. The captain's room, which was carpeted, includes a mahogany bed, a writing table, a bookcase, and a sofa covered with velvet. The 1st, 2nd, 3rd, 4th Officers all have their own rooms, as does the 1st and 2nd engineers.*
>
> *A large deckhouse amidships contains a number of second-class staterooms and lavatories. Its forward section houses a library, paneled in oak. The library is furnished with easy chairs, lounges, writing and occasional tables, and bookcases. Aft of the staterooms, in another deckhouse, is the smokeroom, paneled in walnut. A central skylight provides both light and ventilation.*
>
> *The dining saloon, capable of seating over 200, is located on the shelter deck. It extends the entire width of the ship and is paneled in ivory and white enamel and gold. There is an electrically lit central dome with a stained-glass crown. Above that an exhaust fan for ventilation.*
>
> *Most third-class sleeping accommodations are on the main deck, with the rest on the upper deck. They consist of two and four-berth rooms, all painted white.*
>
> *The third-class dining saloon can be found about amidships on the upper deck. The walls are paneled in polished oak with a teak ornamentation, and the floor was linoleum. The saloon can seat over 300 passengers. Its tables and revolving chairs are*
>
> *Unupholstered hardwood.*

> *Just forward of the saloon on the starboard side is a ladies' room which is furnished with settees, chairs, and occasional tables. A smoke room for male passengers is located on the port side. Forward of them is a fine promenade deck, which could be used in bad weather.*

So, while the *Carpathia* will never aspire to the luxury or the accolades of speed records like the *Mauretania* or *Lusitania* of the Cunard Line, she will treat her passengers well. She can never hope to compete with the promised opulence of hulls # 400 & 401 for the White Star Line now being built in Belfast by Harland & Wolff. They were expected to revolutionize the Atlantic steamship trade. Even their projected names show their ambitions, the *Olympic* and *Titanic*.

As she puts out to sea – Cunard's distinctive flag with the gold lion holding the globe on a red field stiff in the breeze - the topside portion of the 300-person crew and hardy passengers get a last glimpse of land at Bishop's Rock. Standing 49 meters tall, the curved granite lighthouse on Bishop's Rock has been protecting and guiding mariners since 1858. Its Chance Brothers light gives guidance to ships and reassurance to all that the light has somehow survived the pounding storms that break over the tiny granite outcropping regularly. If it can survive the tantrums of the sea, the passengers can as well. Now the *Carpathia* truly starts on her journey; towards Finisterre. Named by the Romans, Finisterre is the far end of the Iberian Peninsula and the end of the earth to those early Romans. Ship routine becomes familiar as the ship churns quietly along towards Lisbon and then the mass of Gibraltar guarding the entrance to the Mediterranean Sea.

7:30 a.m. the first gong of the day sounds for the second and third-class passengers. A bugle blares for the first-class passengers. And the day begins. Breakfast at 8:00 and then a general perambulation around the deck as the plans for the day are made. Each class of passengers seems endlessly fascinated by the other classes so there is always a group at the rail separating passenger classes with gawkers lining the rail. The postings for menus for the day, sports, concerts, and other pastimes scheduled are reviewed and plans made. Follow the leader, relay races, tug of war, three-legged races, pillow fights, cards and cockfights, and nail driving are highlights of the day. Sightings of whales and dolphins are fascinating and a common activity that all classes enjoy. Evenings, after unforgettable sunsets at sea, are filled with a light supper of snacks at 9:30 and then often singing and more games until lights out at 11:00 p.m. Quiet preparations for any upcoming shore excursions are completed over dinner or in the quiet of the staterooms before lights out. They need to be planned to the last detail as the time on shore is often short with much dashing from site to site to complete the visit to strange shores. On Sundays, the Captain holds religious services, one of the few times that all classes of passengers intermingle, and then a Captain's inspection of the ship with his senior officers. A boat drill is also a common Sunday staple, but no passengers are required to attend. RMS *Carpathia*, with her 18 lifeboats, carries the same number of lifeboats required for all ships over 10,000 tons displacement, no matter their passenger capacity.

Small boats always cluster all around the *Carpathia* and other ships anchored off the famous limestone mass of Gibraltar to make their living off the big ships. Some are tenders scurrying swiftly towards shore and the shops lining the streets at the foot of the massive rock formation. Some hopefully draw up directly to the *Carpathia* to sell their fresh fruit and other offerings. Questions and answers are shouted between sellers and buyers and soon baskets can be seen being hauled up filled with merchandise as other baskets drop down with money for their purchases. After a seemingly short time, breathless voyage passengers are re-boarding the ship from tenders after dashing around the small community to see all the sights in the allotted time ashore. The loud rattle of the anchor chain being brought back into the ship, the vibration of the engines, and the reemergence of black smoke from her single central funnel signal the end of the visit and on to the next port of call. Genoa, Naples, Venice, Fiume, Alexandria, and the rest of the Adriatic stops still await. Passengers to be dropped off and picked up along with cargo to load and unload mean the schedule has to be kept. After all, she is a working ship and not one of those glamorous and famous ships working the Atlantic route exclusively. She needs to earn her keep the hard way.

'La Serenissima'– the most serene - the 'queen of the seas'– 'the city of bridges'– all names for Venice, Italy. Some cargo ships though simply call it 'the dirty city'. One ship– the *Brescia*– that the *Carpathia* had encountered in the past knew Venice as the city of coal dust. On every voyage, one entire hold was reserved for 1,000 tons of coal for delivery to the Italian Naval Station at Venice. James Bisset, the Third Officer, often grumbles this was a shipment of 1,000 tons of coal that makes 2,000 tons of black coal dust that land on everything in sight. Navigating the narrow channel towards Port Lido is always a challenge no matter how many times Captain C.A. Smith – *Carpathia*'s Captain for almost a year now since early 1908 - has sailed these same waters. Approaching the confined waters around Venice contains its special benefits though. Even before docking, the officers can see what familiar faces might be in port. Sister Cunarders, White Star, the German steamship lines, or familiar cargo ships like the *Brescia* from the past are searched for to see if friends are in port. The cafes ring with various languages and shimmer with the decorations of the panoply of different seafaring uniforms. Venice affords the world-traveling seamen a popular meeting spot.

The glow of the late afternoon sun slowly lifts its light up the sides of the buildings surrounding the piazza. The unique mix of scents particular to Venice fills the air; strong powerful coffees, overheated seamen on holiday, different and intriguing foods, and above all the waters of the canals. Captain Smith has greeted his friends from the *Brescia* Captain Rostron and Third Officer Bisset. He has already endured the subtle sneering from the waiter at any Venetian café that they receive each time when ordering good English tea instead of the dark Italian coffee. The Italians will never understand the truly civilized virtues of the English or their tea.

The Café Florian – known for its exquisite view since 1720 – occupies a treasured spot in Piazza San Marco. From their tables, diners and drinkers can see the mouth-gaping ornamentation of the domes, arches, and spires of the Basilica of Saint Mark. While the exterior is awe-inspiring and so different from some of the bleak British and Scots churches, the mosaics of the interior were what gave it the nickname of Chiesa d'Oro–Church of Gold. As the day eases along, the sun catches only the top of the domes and famous horses on the loggia. a set of Roman bronze statues of four horses, originally part of a monument depicting a four-horse carriage used for chariot racing. The horses were placed on St Mark's after the sack of Constantinople in 1204. They remained there until looted by Napoleon in 1797 but were returned in 1815.

The customs of the officer's rank are relaxed in these rare moments on shore, even though Bisset is still unbearably uncomfortable following the custom of using last names only for the Captains. He mostly stays out of the conversation to ease the need to address his superiors as Rostron or Smith. They are sitting comfortably at a small table set atop the herring bone patterned stone floor of the piazza. Barricades and scaffolding still surround the unfinished Campanile. The soaring bell tower had collapsed in a pile of bricks suddenly in 1902, miraculously only killing a cat. The reconstruction has been underway almost since the day after the collapse. The Café Florian is a bit expensive for Third Officer Bisset but is a meeting place known to all seamen who frequent Venice and 'meet me at the Florian' is a common message sent from ship to ship.

Rostron is still enjoying the elevated status of his first command. Command of his own had been a dream of his since his youth in Lancashire. He had experienced a taste of command on being named Chief Officer of *Lusitania* until just before she took her maiden voyage. Now it was his time for the real thing. A dream realized. One half the length and one-third the speed of *Lusitania*; the *Brescia* still carries the exalted status of his first command.

"We stop in about 20 ports per voyage all through the Mediterranean and the Adriatic loading and unloading various cargos. All my officers usually work from 7:00 a.m. to 6 p.m. when we work cargo, but often it is simply work until the work is done. Isn't that right Mr. Bisset?"

"Yes sir. Still, I don't mind the work and it is a relief to be off the submarine steamers."

"Ah yes, the ones so low in the water that in any sea at all, you are mostly submerged while standing watch."

"Yes sir."

After the familiar discussion about the quality of the food and English tea in Italy, the conversation turns inevitably to the news of the trade. New innovations in steamship construction and operation are being introduced almost daily. Both the *Brescia* and the *Carpathia* had been launched in 1903 and are seeing their new sisters of the sea bypass them in technology, speed, and comfort. Still, Captain Smith would never dream of trading the lucrative and enjoyable *Carpathia* for another ship. Just as Captain Rostron would not trade his first command for any of the new glamorous fliers being built. The talk goes back and forth on the merits or risks of the new White Star Olympic Class ships which emphasize luxury and opulence over speed and the stout, but expensive, double hull construction the Cunarders feature. The merits of more comfort versus better performance in an unlikely collision are always hotly debated. The value of the new Marconi Wireless technology is also questioned. Some say because of its limited range, eyesight is still the best warning system. It will have little value except to send messages to and from the super rich on the luxury liners.

"Ah but Capt. Rostron, remember just back in January, over 1,700 people were rescued at sea when the S.S. *Republic* collided with the Italian steamer *Florida* in thick fog off the United States East Coast. For two days in freezing conditions Jack Binns, the Marconi radio operator aboard the *Republic*, sent out two hundred messages to help guide rescuing ships to his stricken vessel's position. Thanks to his messages, all but those passengers killed by the initial impact were rescued."

"You are right Bisset. See there, Smith? This young man is going places at sea. He is right up on the latest and a tremendous help to me. He is quite keen on this Marconi process and even visited one of their shore offices at home to learn a bit about it all. This young man will go far in Cunard. Do I see the rank of Cunard commodore in his future?"

"You just might Rostron. You just might."

The seamen could feel the tentative presence of another drawing near to their table attracted by the naval uniforms. A young man approaches; quiet and polite, and yet with a confident manner. "Excuse me, gentlemen. This is my first time in Italy. Can you assist me in ordering bites of food and drink?" This was all said in broken English, with long groping pauses while searching for words and grammar. A small man, with a clean-shaven face and a crisp new uniform. Dark blue with ten gold buttons up the front. A small award ribbon of some kind on the left chest.

"Meine namen ist Wilhelm Werner. Ummm… my name ist Wilhelm Werner."

"Certainly, umm."

"Leutnant…You would say, Lieutenant."

"We usually dispense with rank at the café, Lieutenant. If that is ok with you, we will call you Werner and would be happy to help you. Please join us."

"Danke meine Freunde."

"You are most welcome. What brings you to Venice, Werner?"

"I have just graduated from naval school and am on holiday. I must return soon to my home and then report for duty."

"And where is home, Lieutenant?"

"Alpolda, which is near Weimar in central Germany."

"What naval school did you graduate from young man?"

"Maybe I should not tell you. Will I still be welcome at your table?"

"Why wouldn't you be welcome?

"I just graduated from U-Boat training school. It is all very new and quite dangerous. My father Max is a very conservative prosecutor in my hometown and was quite against me following this line in my career. I will not even tell you – even though you might guess – what my mother thinks. She worries."

"We are all men of the sea. All of our mothers worry."

"Well, it is not a secret, so I guess I can tell you, after a short time at home, I will report on board the U-1. The very first Unterseeboot. We have a crew of 22 and in tests have submerged down to almost 100 feet. I am still getting used to the close quarters and being under the water, but I think I will like it. It is new and challenging. I shall have the means to make my mark. Following the traditional path in the Kaiser's navy is a very slow climb to promotion and command. I do not wish to wait."

"Ah, another young man in a hurry. Eh Bisset?"

"Quite so sir. And good for him I say."

"Becoming impatient Mr. Bisset?"

"No sir. I know I have to wait my turn. But I must confess, while we are here relaxing and off the record I assume, that I will welcome a return to the passenger trade after the umm–shall we say–glamour of the cargo routes wears off."

"Smith, I think the young man means when the coal dust washes off."

"You are right Rostron. That is exactly what he means, and who can blame him?"

"I am sorry Werner. I don't know that we have made our introductions completely, and I can tell we are smashing through this conversation in English and leaving you behind. My name is James Bisset, and I am the Third Officer of the *Brescia*. This is my Captain, Arthur Rostron also of the *Brescia*, and the gentleman over there is Captain C.A. Smith of the RMS *Carpathia*. When we find ourselves in the same port at the same time, we tend to relax the chain of command that is so firmly set on board ship and to let our conversations perhaps relax a bit. Maybe a bit too far at times some of these fellows tell me. I must say it is especially relaxing this time as it seems like every attractive woman in Venice is out and about. No wonder Casanova called this café his hunting ground. This was the only café in Venice that originally allowed women. Looking at these beautiful ladies parading by anyone can see they should have been allowed in wherever they chose"

"Ah so. Actually, I find it relaxing, both the women and the lack of worry about rank. That is one mark of the new U-Boat service I have found already. With only 22 men in that tiny tube, it is more relaxed and with a strong sense of camaraderie not found in the surface fleet. Some of that comes from the common danger, but also the shared challenge of being in a new and elite group."

"Well Werner, as officers of British flagged vessels and also reserve Royal Navy officers, we most earnestly hope that your service in the U-Boats will never be more than training."

"As do I Captain Rostron."

"I have had two distant brushes with war and have no desire for another. First the Boer War and then the heightened tensions during the Russo-Japanese War, and I can't see how anyone benefited on either side from either of those two scraps. Right now, all I can hope for is for the current peace we are enjoying continuing, and possibly a Captainship of a passenger liner for the Cunard Line like the one Captain Smith holds now. Let us just sail the seas in peace."

"Amen."

"Amen."

"Amen."

The soggy night air films the emptying tables in the café as the night deepens. The talk turns back to day-to-day talk of work, family, and news of their shared occupation. The three British mariners debate the positives and negatives of the great ships now being built in Belfast, Ireland at Harland and Wolff. The two ships now under construction will be, by far, the largest in the White Star fleet, and the largest ships afloat. J. Bruce Ismay and the American financier J. Pierpont Morgan have decided to face the challenge from the fastest passenger liners afloat from Cunard –*Lusitania*, and *Mauretania* – by commissioning ships that would surpass the Cunarders not in speed but in size and luxury. The last word in comfort, style, and luxury. Bisset agrees they will be luxurious for the upper class, but points out that to afford more pampering, they have forgone the double hull construction favored for safety by the Cunard Line. He was never in favor of sacrificing any margin of safety in ship construction.

"No ship is unsinkable. Anyone who says that is so is simply speaking from either ignorance or hubris."

Werner made as if to speak on that point but subsided back into his chair silently deciding it was not politic to speak of ships sinking.

"Well, my friends, Mr. Bisset and I need to return to the *Brescia*. We sail at dawn and must attend to our ship. And you, Captain Smith I believe sail with *Carpathia* in the morning as well."

"Indeed, I do Captain Rostron. We have a few more ports before Alexandria in Egypt, and then home. And what of you Leutnant Werner?"

"I have a few more days on holiday before taking the train back to Germany."

"Safe travels to us all then. We part company here until the next time. Good luck on your training Wilhelm."

"And safe voyages to you all. Goodbye Gentlemen."

Dawn had barely broken, and the mists were still rising from the still waters of the Venice lagoon in the morning as the inexpressibly satisfying sound and feel of *Carpathia*'s two Wallsend 8-cylinder quadruple expansion engines came rumbling to life with a promise of new adventures. Her new passengers are still sleeping in the comparative quiet and comfort of their new surroundings. Cabins on the higher decks than other ships for the second and third-class passengers take away much of the pounding engine sounds and turbulence so common in other immigrant trade steamships. *Carpathia* is a lady in all ways and made to pamper even the people considered by many to be the least deserving. The two masts and single funnel of the early-departing *Brescia* are already combined into a distant smudge on the horizon as *Carpathia* navigates the channel towards the open sea. New ports of call await her arrival. New passengers and new cargos to be loaded and some of her current compliment unloaded. She makes her way to her maximum speed of 14 knots and points her prow towards new lands.

Palermo - that stronghold of the mafia in Italy – with the famous "Fountain of Shame" with its' male nude sculptures, and the exquisite Monreale Cloisters wait to be explored in the short time spent ashore for passengers. Fiume - with its vast polyglot of nationalities and languages - is the departure point for many immigrants from both Italy and Hungary. The incredible approach to Malta between Fort St Elmo and Fort Ricasoli, and then to anchor under the commanding presence of Fort Angelo set right in the center of the harbor always provides a fairytale scene. Naples – one of the oldest continuously inhabited cities in the world teems with history and a population living under the constant threat of Vesuvius once again roaring to life and obliterating their homes. Under the ever-present danger of the volcano, many in Naples cope by dedicating themselves to la dolce vita; the good life. Algiers – always a highlight for many passengers as the culture, architecture, and population are completely different from anything in their past experience. No poor Hungarian passengers from the distant farms have ever heard anything like the calls to worship rolling over the city from the tall minarets and it is endlessly fascinating. The passengers are by now accustomed to the patterns of the ship, its rhythms, and habits. Meals, games, concerts, and endless gaping at the new sensations of sea and seaports fill the days.

Shortly after leaving Palermo, the Black Hand symbol of the Mafia begins to appear painted on the white woodwork of the third-class cabin level. The Captain orders it immediately painted over, but the sign appears again in different places painted on the woodwork throughout the ship. Then it was known without a doubt that *Carpathia* was carrying some of the infamous secret society members to new lands where they could spread their influence. Only one culprit is caught and even the usually effective discipline method is ineffective against the power of the Black Hand. He refuses to identify his fellow "artists" even after a few days and nights down in the darkest, coldest hold of the ship where the only company is the unceasing pounding of the waves and the hammering of the ship's engines, along with the constant scrabbling of the scurrying rats. Normally after a day or two of that treatment, any miscreant acknowledges the error of their ways and refrains from any further misdeeds. But against the power and threat of the Mafia, the normal methods weighed against the health, safety, and life itself of the one caught, make the decision to stay silent an easy one.

The noise from the 'howling dervishes' as the Captain called the stevedores, fortune tellers, city guides, and hucksters that descend on the Carpathia when she docks at Alexandria, Egypt is always deafening. Moored comfortably at the dock in New Harbor, she lets her passengers file down the long ramps to solid ground as the deck crew sweats unloading cargo. She will rest here a couple of days as the passengers explore the ancient city, while loads of baled cotton, cottonseed, and onions refill her cargo holds. Captain Smith, while not a pilgrimage, always finds time to visit the Cathedral of St. Catherine the martyr whenever he is in Alexandria. He always thinks the church is almost a twin to Sant' Andrea della Valle in Rome; a favorite of his when visiting that Italian city. He loves the look of the paired columns on the exterior and the exquisite ornamentation of the interior. Plus, the life of St. Catherine is so compelling and faith inspiring. Catherine was a young woman who experienced a vision of the Madonna and child during the reign of Emperor Maximian. She boldly went to the emperor and argued with him about his cruelty to her fellow Alexandrians. The emperor brought the best pagan philosophers to debate her Christian principles, but Catherine prevailed. Several of those pagans converted on the spot and were put to death by the emperor. She was imprisoned but continued to convert even in jail, including the emperor's wife who was then killed as well. Catherine was then beheaded, and it is said angels carried her body to Sinai. Her unswerving faith, no matter what horrible fates awaited her, always renewed the Captain no matter the number of times he visited the church. The Captain is a man of deep faith as are many mariners who trust their lives to the elements on the sea.

"Hello, Captain Smith."

"Hello. Who…"

"Cottam, sir. Harold Cottam. We met in Liverpool. I was mostly working installing the Marconi system on Russian ships at the time but had to make a brief visit to your ship as well. I work for Guglielmo Marconi."

"Oh yes, young man, I remember you now. Why are you in Alexandria?"

"Well sir, my ship the *Medic*, threw a propeller blade off Suez and I had a bit of time to travel as we wait for the replacement."

"Well, this is a nice surprise. I had thought you told me you were going to work at the General Post Office in Liverpool in their telegraph room."

"I had sir. I found that the work on shore in those surroundings a bit much for me. That giant building with its various mazes of rooms and hallways; the statuary representing England, Scotland, Ireland, and Wales, a whole floor for the kitchens and dining room for the staff; all the marble and mahogany. It was all somewhat intimidating. So, I decided to take advantage of the simpler life and surroundings back at sea. I am sure you of all people can understand. I did have a chance to go back to the Marconi school at Beaconsfield house, but I wished to be back out on my own. There is no chance for adventure in a post office or school."

"And you think that the small Marconi shack on a small ship like the *Medic* will give you that chance Mr. Cottam?"

"Well Captain, it might not. However, I am here in the home of one of the wonders of the ancient world–the great lighthouse of Alexandria–and the catacombs of Kom al Shaggafa, Pompey's pillar, the Great Library of Alexandria, and ….."

"Enough Mr. Cottam! I see your point. I wouldn't be a ship

Captain if I didn't agree."

"Thank you, sir. Plus, right now that are so few of us experienced Marconi operators that I have great hopes for the future. We operators are really a small exclusive club."

"I don't know how you young men do it. That small room with the noise, smell, smoke, and gas from the transmitters and batteries must be hard to work in. Not to mention the actual spark and heat from the transmitter itself."

"Well, sir, I like the newness of the technology. I shouldn't brag, but I was the youngest to go through the Marconi school and in the shortest time as well, so I took to the noise and risk and all that goes with it. Plus Mr. Marconi is making improvements all the time so that is very exciting as well."

"Well, Mr. Marconi must be proud of you."

"I haven't met him as yet but hope to one day."

"Speaking of meeting people, Mr. Cottam. Please forgive my manners. I have two people with me that I would like you to meet. This is Reverend Allen Hadnot, lately of India, and his daughter Elizabeth."

"Harold Cottam, Reverend Hadnot."

Reverend Allen was a slight man, barely taller than Harold who stands 5'5". Burned brown by the sun, he looks a bit worn but graceful in his movements. Command presence, it is called in the military or at sea, combined with a sense of gentleness that found its expression in his direct glance and gentle handshake. Hands calloused by hard work, his grip is still gentle and concerned for the well-being of the other. Behind him, partially shielded, appears a girl of about 10 years. Wheat blond hair, impossibly slight, and with eyes the color of the blue glacial ice found in the North Atlantic. She shyly extends her hand in greeting.

"And this is my daughter, Miss Elizabeth Ruth Hadnot."

Harold flinches a bit under a direct gaze so unusual for a 10-year-old. Without seeming invasive, she catalogs in great detail Harold's wavy hair, slightly crooked smile, long jaw, the nervous energy just under the surface, and his erect small man's posture. Even though eight years older, Harold is the one to flush red and turn away. Elizabeth's father is either completely unaware or simply used to his daughter's effects on people. Especially young men.

"Reverend Hadnot is a missionary in India nearing the end of a short combination of business visit and a holiday for his daughter. I met them at Pompey's Pillar and I was able to guide them to the church which was next on their list of sights to visit."

"Harold is one of those new Marconi men who send and take the wireless messages. It is quite new. For myself, I would think that nothing sent by wireless could be any better than a good seaman can see for himself. Sorry Mr. Cottam, I do not mean to demean your work."

"Not at all Captain. I understand we are a new service. However, the story of the *Republic* has already shown the possibilities for the Marconi system."

"Ahh yes Cottam, I suppose it does. However..."

The tiny voice of Elizabeth breaks in with a question about what the *Republic* was.

"Well, Elizabeth and Reverend Hadnot, I would not suppose you would have heard the story in India. It was big news both in England and America though. Right on January 23 of this year, one of the largest of the great steamers, the RMS *Republic* of the White Star line was traveling in thick fog off the coast of Nantucket in America, when the SS *Florida* crashed into her amidships–right in the middle of the ship I mean–and she began to sink. One of our boys–Jack Binns–got right about sending a message to any and all ships in the area asking for help. CQD....CQD....THIS IS MKC....CQD....CQD. You see folks when I tap out CQ on the wireless pad, that means attention all ships, and then adding the D means distress. The MKC is the 'name' of the ship. So, our boy Jack sends that message over and over and over. Ships begin to gather from everywhere. So, although the Republic did sink, good old boy Jack was able to help ships like the *Baltic* get there in time to save over 1,500 people counting both passengers and crew. That is a smashing success for the Marconi system. Wouldn't you say so, Captain Smith?"

"Well yes, son, yes, it is. However, there was still a collision, and the ship did still sink, didn't it? And the lifeboats ferried the passengers to other ships as designed, didn't they?"

Harold quite visibly swallows further words knowing that the circle of Captains on the great steamships are all quite close and reputations can be made or broken with an intemperate word. He might end up forever on small cargo steamers if he allows his defense of the new technology to become too heated. Mentioning that steaming in fog and crashing into another ship might be a bit more of a seamanship issue rather than a wireless one might be accurate but not politic. Pointing out again that the other ships wouldn't have come to *Republic*'s aid in that same fog without the wireless summons would not be welcome either. He can already see that the Captain's face had reddened under his thick white beard. Harold recalls hearing from other operators of Smith's temper when provoked. Making a swift tactical career-preserving retreat, Harold turns the conversation to the Hadnot family.

"So Reverend, tell me of your work in India."

"Well Reverend Hadnot, and young Mr. Cottam, my ship will be sailing on the afternoon tide so I must get back to her. There is still much to do. I will leave you to your stories. Safe travels to you all."

"And to you Captain. I hope to see you and the *Carpathia* again soon. Thank you for the escort."

Finding a small café just outside the Arab village near the ruins of one of the great ancient gates of the city, the group settles in with Elizabeth finding a place near Harold. Soon in distinctive clear glasses of uncertain cleanliness, the Bedouin tea arrives with its accompanying sugar, milk, and lemon. This café has always been known for its special blend of marmaraya leaves and the distinctive taste of its tea. In the center of the small uneven table, a plate of the sweet treat Lugmet el Gadi waits to be sampled.

"Try one Elizabeth. It is a small round dough ball crunchy on the outside and filled with sweet syrup inside and dusted with a light coating of cinnamon. They are delicious and a favorite of the locals here. I first tried one only a few days ago in Suez, and they are very tasty. You will enjoy it."

"It is alright Elizabeth. I think we can trust young Mr. Cottam."

"Alright, father." A small voice–even smaller than the thin frame it comes from. A tiny smile growing into a larger one rewards Harold, along with a glance that is somehow disconcerting.

"Well young Mr. Cottam, what would you like to know about our ministry in India?"

"I have yet to be on the India run, so I don't know much about the country and what you do there."

Taking off his bowler, Reverend Hadnot wipes his balding head with a startlingly red handkerchief and speaks with quiet pride of his work for the United Lutheran Church mission. Located in the southeast part of India, Guntur was situated on the plains about 40 miles north of the Bay of Bengal. A far 875 miles to New Delhi where there is talk of moving the capital and about 800 miles from Calcutta, Guntur is an area about as isolated from western influence as possible. They still fight cholera and smallpox using the old ways of the local Kabiraj and their old Sanskrit texts. One of the greatest struggles in that part of India is snakes. In a recent year across India, over 20,000 people had died from snake bites alone.

Looking at Elizabeth, Hadnot says "That is a constant fear and battle for Elizabeth, her mother, and I at the mission. We run an orphanage as part of our mission and making sure we don't lose any of our littlest ones to snakes is a constant battle."

The Hadnots are originally from a western farming area of Ohio in America. Reverend Hadnot had married his wife Nellie in 1895 and Elizabeth was born nine months to the day later in India. In the years since coming to India the mission had grown and after the great famine of 1900, the demand for spaces in the orphanage next to the church they had built multiplied ten times. Now their St. Matthew Church, the orphanage, and their garden take every minute of every day and have developed in the missionary a practical outlook on everyday life. He has seen much death, sadness, and everyday struggle and it has leavened some of his original missionary zeal. Now his missionary work consists of the day-to-day actions of his family rather than a strict application of doctrines.

"That sounds very demanding Reverend."

"It is. But it is also very rewarding. I won't go into the whole story, but the success we have had at the orphanage is truly a victory of life over death. Actually, we are here in Alexandria for a mixed purpose relating to life over death. I did need to have a meeting or two while here, but mostly it is a holiday for this young one who recently had her own brush with death."

"Snakes?"

"No, not this time. Elizabeth and some of the young orphans were playing in the River Krishna nearby and we almost lost Elizabeth to drowning. It was all over quickly and neither Nellie nor I were there, so we are still a bit unsure how the trouble started, but we are very blessed to still have our little girl with us. So, her mother and I decided to give her a bit of a holiday from her work and explore this ancient city that has always intrigued me. Her mother didn't feel that she could leave the mission without one of us there, so she stayed behind. So very soon, we shall find our *Peninsular and Orient* steamer and start the long journey home. In fact, we should be on our way. This has been very pleasant young man."

"Yes, Reverend. I have enjoyed it as well. My train from here to Cairo and then on to Suez doesn't leave until later today, but I should be on my way as well. I have enjoyed meeting you and hope to see you somewhere again in the future and perhaps meet your wife. And you Miss Hadnot, I have enjoyed meeting you. Is she always this quiet?"

"Oh my no. She is usually quite the chatterbox. Perhaps you have had a salutary influence on her."

A quick blush from young Elizabeth. A glance up at her father and she extends her small hand for a very grown-up goodbye.

As Harold leaves the port area to catch his train, he spies the distinctive tall funnel spewing out a stream of black smoke as the *Carpathia* leaves the channel and stands out to sea.

"Someday, I will see you again. I swear it."

Chapter 2

FATEFUL JOURNEY

She has sailed thousands and thousands of miles since her maiden voyage under Captain James C. Barr in April 1903. Voyages taken under Captain 'Bowler Bill' Turner and other Captains. Thousands of miles and thousands of passengers. Now she lies resting alongside Pier 54 in the shadow of the soaring skyscrapers of New York City at the end of March 1912. She knows she has rested here long enough. The familiar wanderlust is returning as her bunkers fill with coal. It has taken a full day and a half to complete the coal bunkering to sustain her on her next trip, but now she is full, eager, and ready. It has been cold and damp with a light dusting of snow in New York. Spring has been only a rumor as she lay lifeless along the great pier, and she is yearning for warmer temperatures. Today though is different. The welcome sunshine is eagerly absorbed as it penetrates between the tall towers to fill the dark corners of *Carpathia*. It has come very late this year but now Crocus weather, as some on land called it, has finally arrived. The flowers that arrive with the first promise of warm spring weather are making their tentative exploration above ground. Even the harbor air smells warmer. The decks pulse now with the sound of footfalls and the first wisps of smoke float out of her funnel into the clear sky. She is alive again!

RMS *Carpathia* departed the Huskisson dock, into the River Mersey on February 10, 1912, starting the four-day trip from Liverpool to Gibraltar. From Gibraltar, she sailed for Algiers and Malta. February 22nd found her in Alexandria, Egypt, and then off to Constantinople and Trieste. Trieste will mark the end of her outbound trip and the unloading of passengers and cargo. From now on, her holds and cabins will be filling with cargo and passengers for her return trip. At Trieste she takes on 595 tons of cargo and 151 passengers; at Fiume another 300 tons of cargo and 754 human cargo and at Sicily 37 more passengers and 382 tons in her holds.

Palermo and Naples gave her 148 more souls and 424 more tons of goods. Three mornings later, her engines are silenced for the last time before leaving the waters of the Mediterranean Sea as she loads her final 28 passengers at Gibraltar. Now she begins her longest stretch alone at sea – 11 days to America. As one of her officers likes to recall "It was then that the fun really began" for the passengers seeing the vast unfeeling swells of the Atlantic ocean spreading out in front of them. She arrives off Sandy Hook, New York on March 29th and after the customary health inspection, she is welcomed home into her accustomed berth along the Manhattan waterfront.

Her home - the massive complex of the Chelsea piers and Pier 54 have welcomed the great steamships for years now and seethed with a life and energy unlike any other. Passengers, crew members, cargo handlers, and the usual crowds of people trying to make a living feeding off those same people both in legal and other ways swarm. Above the crowds and confusion, the massive brick facades with the huge CUNARD and WHITE STAR names welcome the liners and their passengers. Architects Warren & Wetmore were celebrated for their design of the piers with their combination of the grandiose design hard-scrapple function. Now complete, they were turning their design talents to their next big project, tentatively named Grand Central Station. The massive granite face of each pier head was graced by a signature front arched window supported by a colossal steel arch concealed with stone. Just above the CUNARD word on the front soared the open pediment supported by massive corbels. Each pediment had two stone figures supporting a globe at its peak showing the approaching passengers the worldwide reach across the oceans of the great steamships.

The ten days that *Carpathia* has rested until now alongside Pier 54 discharging and loading cargo has allowed for rest, relaxation, filling crew needs, and sightseeing of all kinds. On one of his off days, newly appointed Second Officer Bisset did some sightseeing with a short walk to Pier 59. The giant super liner *Olympic* – the first of her class of three ships – had arrived in New York harbor and Bisset availed himself of the opportunity to make a short courtesy visit and explore the ship that dwarfed everything else along the piers. Seated in the small mess room with fellow junior officers Dean and Rees, he made his report. "Her promenade deck is a quarter mile around. The bridge is 100 feet from starboard to port and her boat deck 100 feet above the waterline. Colossal! Awe-inspiring! To me though, I wonder if it is too big to handle, but I am probably just not experienced enough as yet. The officer that showed me the ship was supremely confident both in her handling and in her durability. The officer – I cannot recall his name – said she was unsinkable. She has 16 watertight bulkheads and watertight doors which could be closed electrically by pressing a button on the bridge. She has a double bottom. But I wonder why they didn't build her with the double skin on the sides of her hull as the *Mauretania* and *Lusitania* had. Was it to save cost or are they so confident in their hulls of riveted steel plates? I assume that they have supreme confidence that if needed, the watertight compartments would provide enough buoyancy if needed in an emergency. I must say, Rees, that when I mentioned that the compartments didn't extend up to the deckheads and that in an emergency the water could overflow from one compartment to another, the young *Olympic* officer just dismissed me as a young know-nothing. Perhaps he is right. Still, I would be more confident shipping on a White Star if I knew it had the double hulls. Perhaps I am just both a bit of a worrier and also superstitious. I try not to believe in a ship being cursed with "hoodoo" but certainly no good luck can come to a ship like the new *Titanic* when it completes its sea trials on April Fools Day – hoodoo or not! I know those two Marconi boys on the new ship, and I hope to connect with them as we voyage to see how the new ship is working for them, but I will happily take my new berth here on *Carpathia* at any event."

Each cross-Atlantic voyage brings with it many changes. Changes in passengers and cargo, but also ship's officers and crew. A cross-Atlantic voyage with a Captain new to the ship requires adjustments by the ship itself as it responds to the new hand at the helm, and most visibly, the adjustments being made by the officers and crew to the new personality of the ship determined by the Captain.

Arthur Henry Rostron, the new Captain just this January, was born in Bolton, Lancashire England, in 1869. By 1912 he had served in sailing ships around Cape Horn, years as a junior officer in various Cunarders, and then Chief Officer in the *Pannonia* on her maiden voyage in 1903. Known as a seaman's seaman, he was Chief Officer on the fast liner *Lusitania* on her sea trials, until promoted to his own command on the day before *Lusitania*'s maiden voyage. *Carpathia* is his sixth command and one of his largest. His Second Officer – a February 1912 addition – James Bisset, describes him as a man easy with his seaman's skills, a disciplinarian, and a man who could make a decision quickly and stick to it. Not the type-cast old sea dog, Rostron is a man of a thin and wiry build, sharp features, and piercing blue eyes that could penetrate any unruly crewman. The men throughout the

Cunard service know him as the 'Electric Spark' for his quick decisions and rapid movements – a dynamic person exuding energy in all his professional actions. Strongly religious and austere, he does not drink, smoke, or use profanity. His prayer habits are legendary and respected by all who have served under him. Often, he moves to one side of the wheelhouse, raises his cap a few inches, and quietly stands in silent prayer. He is a man dedicated to his craft and his God. So, while the crew holds his ship-handling skills such as to keep them out of harm's way, some of the less religious – less refined – less inclined to sobriety – look at him closely with a bit of discomfort.

Captain Rostron crowds his officers into his cabin and lines them up near the stairs in front of the bookcase before getting underway. His cabin is a luxurious reward of his new command. Mahogany woods and plush carpets, both a table and a desk, along with a large chart room are all part of his new spacious domain.

"Gentlemen, I wanted to speak with you all before sailing so we are all clear on what we face and the performance I desire and shall expect. First, let me officially introduce everyone: Chief Officer Thomas Hankinson is the gentleman over there with the impressive mustache. First Officer Horace Dean is the older gent there next to Hankinson. Next in line is our new Second Officer. Welcome to the *Carpathia* James Bisset and glad to sail with you again. Third Officer, Eric Rees, and Fourth Officer, Geoffrey Barnish finish up that row. Our Chief engineer, AB Johnstone is that solid-looking man in front, and the slight young man next to him is Purser Ernest Brown. Finally, is the famous, or infamous according to what I have heard, Chief Steward Harry Hughes. Our new Marconi wireless man is in the Marconi shack and his name is Harold Cottam. He shipped on *Carpathia* for a bit in 1911 and we welcome him back to her. Now to those of you new to *Carpathia*, we have three doctors on board - English, Italian, and

Hungarian. Doctor Frank McGhee is our English doctor and surgeon. To his right is Doctor Lengyel for our Hungarian passengers and to his left is Doctor Vittorio Risicato for our Italian passengers."

"Now Gentlemen, we will work together as one. We have had a very large turnover of the crew since we lost about 30 men in Fiume and another 37 have found the temptations of New York City too great for them and they are among the missing as well. So, we sail with approximately twenty percent of our crew new to the *Carpathia*. This is our challenge on this voyage. We must make them *Carpathia* men immediately and this will require your strictest attention. At the same time, remember gentlemen that I require all my officers to participate fully in making the passengers' time on board a memorable one, and you are required to participate in ship-board activities, games, and the like. Be part of the experience in addition to your seaman's duties. Any questions?"

The persistent thrum of noise of ship's preparations - cranes loading cargo, the sounds of lost passenger feat on deck, and the screeching of scavenging gulls - are the only sounds to answer the Captain.

"Now I always share this story at the start of the voyage, so some of you must listen to it again. My apologies. To you new officers, I share this story so there is no inaccurate gossip about this incident, plus also as a warning to be ever vigilant. I plan on taking our passengers and ourselves to our destination and returning safely. At sea, the only way to accomplish such a thing is with an ever-attentive crew."

"When I was Chief Officer on the *Campania* back in '07, we were coming into Queenstown, when off Galley Head, I noticed something sticking out of the water.' Keep clear of that snag ahead,' I called to the junior officer who was with me on the bridge. We swung away a point but gradually drew nearer so that we were able to make out what the unusual thing was. It was a sea monster! It was no more than fifty feet from the ship when we passed it, so both I and the other officer had a good sight of it. So strange an animal was it that I remember calling out 'It's alive!' One has heard of such yarns about these monsters and cocked a speculative eye at the teller that I wished as never before that I had a camera in my hands. Failing that, I did the next best thing and on the white dodger board in front of me, I made sketches of the animal, full face, and profile, for the thing was turning its head from side to side for all the world as a bird will on a lawn between its pecks. I was unable to get a clear view of the monster's features, but we were close enough to realize its head rose eight or nine feet out of the water, while the trunk of the neck was fully twelve inches thick. The other officer, H.C. Birnie, corroborated the entire thing, but my Captain didn't believe either one of us. He asked me what I had drunk with dinner that night! I had to remind him that I didn't drink. Even coming back after shore leave, the Captain asked me again 'Did you see it, Rostron?' However, the previous evening at home I was looking at the evening paper and read of an experience that a man had gone through in the Bristol Channel. He had gone out fishing in the evening and had been attacked by a huge sea monster and had fought it off with his boathook and oars, losing them all. His description of the animal compared accurately with the one I had seen, and, as I saw it heading from the south of Ireland in the direction of the Bristol Channel, there as little doubt in my mind that it was the same - and no longer any doubt in the Captain's mind that my monster had been real enough. Or to my sobriety for that matter. So, you see gentlemen, there are many wonders and dangers we might see in our sailing of the seas. Keep your eyes on a good lookout at all times. As I said, and I know you join with me, I plan to bring our ship, passengers, and crew safely to their destinations and home again. So once again, sirs, keep a keen lookout at all hazards. Incidentally, gentlemen, we will have an extra lookout to protect us besides those of us standing here. While I was on the *Campania* it became the second ship in the Cunard fleet to have wireless capability, and I had learned to value the extra sets of eyes coming from other ships on our route reporting to us by wireless. As I said, Mr. Cottam - our Marconi man - is one of the new men joining our ship, as is Mr. Bisset here. However, while I know there are some that do not yet see the value of Marconi's magic, and think what can possibly hurt us that we cannot see with our own eyes across the vastness of the sea, we will heed the information he gives us. He will be treated as a valued member of this crew, even if he is actually employed by Mr. Marconi. I would charge you younger officers to spend some time with him. Do not distract him from his work, but wireless will be very important as the years go by and you would be wise to learn all you can."

"Now to business, you know your duties and the standards of a Cunarder. We will be going to sea with a light load of 734 passengers. We should be able to extend exemplary service to each of them. Let us get to work. We leave as close to noon as possible. Dismissed. Mr. Bisset, a moment please."

Rostron moves to his desk as the other officers file out. "Mr. Bisset, I know you have many duties as Second Officer, but I would like to ask a bit of personal privilege. Music is a passion of mine, and our passengers often evaluate the entire voyage on the music provided to them on board. Our piano player, Theodore Brailey, and our cello player, Roger Bricoux, have transferred from our ship to the new *Titanic* for its maiden voyage. I could not hold them as they decided that the super liner *Titanic* was a much better opportunity for them. Can you oversee the new orchestra members and make sure they get acclimated? Often the musicians and Marconi men don't fully feel like members of the crew due to them being employed by either their Liverpool agents or directly by the Marconi Company. Mr. Cottam has been on board before so he should not require special attention. Also, we have a brand-new bugler who is on his first voyage and is very young. Let's see, his name is Mr. A. McLean. New seamen of his age often require a steadying hand that I would ask you to provide from time to time. Make them feel welcome as part of our crew."

"Yes sir, with pleasure."

"You know Mr. Bisset, even the new orchestra director on the *Titanic* used to be a shipmate with me while on the *Lusitania*. Everyone seems drawn to the new, bigger, faster ships. To my mind, not necessarily better though, but I need to keep my own counsel about that. Sometimes we just don't know what the better opportunity in life truly is. Now your cabin is port side, and you are near Mr. Rees. I am sure you found your accommodations quite a change from what we had the last time we shipped together. If you have not finished getting your gear stowed away, please step to it and report back to me here."

"Yes sir. Thank you, sir."

On the other side of the Atlantic, also at about noon, two massive 38-ton propellers churn the water quayside in Queenstown. Aboard the RMS *Titanic* – the largest man-made moving object on earth - are 1,390 passengers, including some of the richest people in the world, a crew of over 900, and 3,814 sacks of mail. John Jacob Astor IV and his much younger bride, the mining heir Benjamin Guggenheim, Isidor Straus of Macy's Department Store fame, a military aide to the United States President and so many other luminaries of the upper class were on board that the combined wealth of the first class on this journey was upwards of 500 million dollars. Truly the crème de le crème of polite society. The fabulously rich J.P. Morgan was rumored to have booked cabin B 52 but changed his plans and was not on board. Guglielmo Marconi was offered free passage on the *Titanic* but preferred the stenographer on the *Lusitania* to help him with his work on the voyage so took that ship three days earlier. All classes of passengers gape at the luxurious and elaborate appointments throughout the ship. Descending to second-class cabin F4, the Hadnot family is overwhelmed at the pampering they will receive on this voyage. After their sparse living arrangements in India at the mission, this was truly a world apart. So many changes coming to the family in such a short time! After this short watery interlude, what would their new life in Ohio be like? Would the mission continue to thrive without their presence? And the ever-present thought for Mrs. Hadnot, would she and her family be safe on this trip? She had stopped talking about it, but the family knew it was never far from her mind.

Comfortable and friendly, the *Carpathia* carries several honeymooning couples as part of the departing passengers. Emma and Milton Hutchison are recently married, as are Howard and Hope Brown from Rhode Island. James Fenwick and his new bride Mabel confounded the other passengers due to their age. He was 38 and she 33, but are newlyweds, nonetheless. Josephine and Charles Marshall, with their daughter Evelyn are traveling towards their home in Paris, while her nieces will approach them westbound on the *Titanic*. As soon as they come into range of the Marconigrams, she plans to send them a message in the new wireless way. Carlos Hurd is taking a two-month leave of absence from his newspaper reporting job in St. Louis to travel to Europe with his wife Katherine. He has made one dream come true just before boarding. A job interview with the editor of the *New York Evening World*! He had been offered a position, but the long delay of the trip could put that offer in jeopardy. After all, nothing much will happen on this trip and his name is sure to be forgotten by the New York editor in the intervening time. Dr. Frank Blackmarr and his young neighbor companion look forward to exploring every inch of their ship on the passage across the Atlantic. A busybody by nature, Dr. Blackmarr is going to Europe to learn the latest developments in his radiology profession. He and his young neighbor are interested in anything scientific. Others on the ship have destinations for sightseeing, but most of the third-class passengers are looking forward to setting their eyes on home and family across the Atlantic.

Making their way along the decks to the large staircase, they are directed towards one of the large mosaic-tile landings with the large CARPATHIA inset where further directions to their individual cabins would be given by the large staff of stewards. Positive comments are being shared with the voyagers by veteran second and third-class passengers when they arrive at their quarters. Large rooms, excellent ventilation, and fine appointments – so unusual for the less privileged classes in other ships – are a welcome surprise and compare favorably with anything that any previous voyager had seen.

As *Titanic* turns her two massive manganese-bronze propellers – the third only engaged when underway – the colossal turbulence tosses other nearby ships about. The liner *New York* docked and silent at the next pier is buffeted so strongly that she loses her moorings. The snap of her lines can be heard above all other sounds on the quay. She begins to drift towards *Titanic*'s port side. Captain Edward John – commonly nicknamed EJ - was on the bridge with the controlling harbor pilot and he instantly stops his engines allowing the *New York* to swing harmlessly past the *Titanic* with mere feet to spare. This was almost a repeat experience for Captain Smith. September 20, 1911, he had once again been on the bridge with a harbor pilot conning the ship. That time in command of *Titanic*'s sister ship the RMS *Olympic*. Once again, the turbulence and suction caused by the immense power of these new super ships caused havoc in the harbor. Captain Smith did not receive the benefit of good luck on that day. The Royal Navy Voyager HMS *Hawke* heeled over under the strain and rammed into her starboard side just aft of the well deck. Penetrating a full eight feet into the *Olympic*, the *Hawk* tore a 40-foot gash below the waterline. Two of *Olympic*'s compartments immediately flooded and her propeller shaft was bent beyond further use. Sorely wounded, she limped back to Belfast for extensive repairs. She would rest there for weeks as thousands of Belfast's best at Harland & Wolff put her to rights. The *Titanic* – still under construction on the ways – was cannibalized for parts. She gave up a propeller and propeller shaft to Captain Smith's damaged ship which postponed *Titanic*'s launch date by three weeks. White Star made much publicly of how *Olympic* absorbed the damage and was virtually unsinkable. However, no one could know the public relations effects or any other unforeseen consequences that might occur because of *Titanic*'s maiden voyage being pushed back to an uncertain date in April rather than the last week of March. Still, many passengers have complete faith in Captain Smith. He is known to frequent travelers, especially the first-class voyagers who had nicknamed him 'The Millionaires' Captain. But many men who go down to the sea in ships are superstitious and fear the unexpected events that turn on the unlikeliest circumstances. Some of *Titanic*'s officers and crew mumbled quietly about the new super liner being a "hoodoo ship" and worried about the next unlucky occurrence on the unproven ship.

Leaving Southampton, *Titanic* proceeds to Cherbourg where she arrives just after 6:00 p.m. on the 10th of April. There 274 passengers board the ship and 24 disembark at Cherbourg, their trip complete. At 8:00 p.m. she resumes her voyage and heads for Queenstown, Ireland which she reaches the next morning at 11:30 a.m. Anchoring about two miles from shore, 120 passengers board tenders along with 1,385 additional sacks of mail and are loaded aboard the new ship. She weighs anchor and her massive engines rumble once again to live to take her to sea on the great circle route to America on April 11, 1912.

The Marconi shack on the *Carpathia* had been grafted on the raised lifeboat deck aft of the funnel. Sandwiched between two lifeboats on davits and 4 additional 28' collapsible boats, the Marconi shack had been an addition to the original design. The new technology requires aerials, wires, and a home for both all the wireless equipment and the operator himself. The workspace consists of a 'silent room' where all the loud equipment is kept so the noise of the equipment itself won't make it impossible for the operator to hear the signals. An equipment table where the essentials of the wireless key and his notepads are kept, and a desk fills up his workspace. Marconi system equipment mounted on the walls surround the operator covering every inch of his small space. A small separate room contains the essentials of his living space. A hot and noisy space. Only one door for ventilation, and that facing aft. While that did cut down on the smoke from the funnel, it also allowed little sea breeze to enter while underway. Second-class passengers in the smoke room immediately below can clearly hear the crackling and snapping sounds and the clicking of the spark key as they relax in the hazy room below the Marconi house. Harold can be seen at all hours hunched over at his equipment table with his earphones clamped to his head sending messages from passengers, receiving news and messages from shore stations or ships, or gossiping with other Marconi men on ships within range. Being the only operator, he is usually found working any time between 7:00 a.m. and 11:00 p.m. During times of recreation, meals, or overnight, the system is shut down and unattended. When actual Marconigram business was slow, Harold can be seen with his earphones on gossiping with his fellow Marconi men by dots and dashes. Each ship has its own call sign; even though most operators can tell who was operating the set by their style of sending the dots and dashes – their 'fist'. These young men – especially the young British Boys as they were called – as pioneers of their industry are constantly learning and teaching on the job. They have even developed their own private language to be used between themselves.

QRL – Keep quiet, I'm busy

DDD – Shut up

G – Go ahead

K – Please reply

MSG – Prefix to Master's service message Captain must acknowledge

STD Bl – Stand by

NR – No response

GTH – Go to hell

OM – Old man

TUOMGN – Thank you old man, good night

GTHOMQRL – Go to hell old man, keep quiet, I'm busy

ASOM – Wait a minute old man

CQD – All stations distress call

SOS – New distress call just being introduced

Morse code had become universally used for over twenty years and the young Marconi men compete with each other for speed and accuracy on their message keying. The passion and competitiveness they show with their dots and dashes make them seem a bunch of 'cranks' at times to others in the ship's crew. Most of these young operators on various ships know or know of each other. They are a closed club of young men growing up as their young technology is growing up as well.

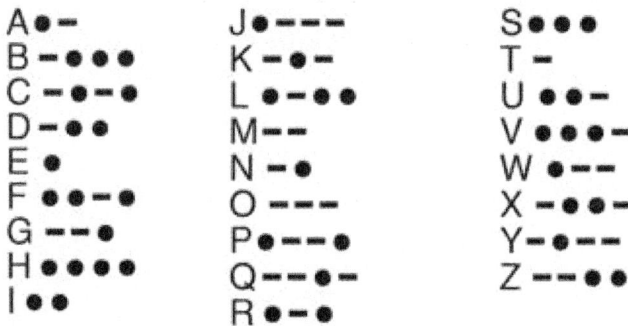

Within hours of leaving America, Dr. Blackmarr and his young protégée have followed the snapping and popping sounds to Harold's Marconi house. Young Cecil is endlessly fascinated by all the equipment mounted to the walls and the sparking and flashing of the Marconi system.

"Cecil, if you and the good doctor want to stop by for a bit each day, I will teach you Morse code. No one but me touches the actual system – Mr. Marconi would have my head on a plate – but I can teach you the letters and some of the secret phrases we operators use to make the job easier. Maybe sometime every day right after lunch when I open up again would be best. If that is acceptable to you, we will start tomorrow."

"Mr. Cottam, you have made this young man's trip. He has a scientific bent of mind, and I hope he will develop that character further. Not very many boys his age want to learn about my radiology equipment, medicine, and other disciplines of the scientific mind. Young Mr. Cecil here is always asking questions about everything and has quite the desire to learn most everything in the various sciences."

"Well, it will be my pleasure Doctor. I was the youngest to go through the Marconi school myself, so I appreciate his curiosity at a young age. I will see you tomorrow then."

As the *Carpathia* follows her route towards the warmth of the Mediterranean, the shipboard routine settles into familiar unremarkable patterns. The two common topics of conversation amongst dinner and promenade companions are the ever-colder weather and the unusually placid seas of the Atlantic in these mid-April days – a time of oft-times stormy weather at sea. Above decks, the passengers converse, read and make small talk. The daily review of the menu is a highlight of the mid-ocean part of the voyage. The luncheon menu contains tempting items like Bordeaux sardines and Norwegian anchovies and ox tail for appetizers. Main courses can feature boiled leg of mutton, lamb chops, and various cold items. Deserts of Rhubarb & Puffs, Chester cakes, and vermicelli pudding finish the afternoon meal. Dinner menus often start with caviar on toast and – for a touch of France - salmi of duckling. Roast spring lamb with mint sauce, calves' head vinaigrette, and roast turkey guarantee something for every taste. Plum pudding, apple tarts, sage puddings, or lemon cheesecakes are only a few of the after-dinner choices. By the third day patterns of dining, walking the ever-colder decks, musical concerts, and the ever-present sports and games are cast in stone. As in all groups, the same people hold to themselves, and the joiners take part in the games and planned activities. Relay races, shuffle board, bull board, nail driving, boot & shoe, potato race, pillow fights, and the always popular amateur nights are in full operation on board. Ship's officers can normally be found taking part in most games, with uneven levels of skill and enthusiasm. Captain Rostron insists his officers be part of the activities to enhance the experience for his passengers so uniformed Cunard officers are performing most games, sing-a-longs, and other group activities alongside the passengers with disparate ability levels.

Behind closed doors and below public decks the business of operating the great liner continues unseen 24 hours a day. Deep inside her heart, trimmers, stokers, and firemen work at their dark and dusty duties. The members of the 'black gang' work to power the heart of the ship. Moving tons of coal into the coal chutes and then leveling the vast piles of coal to evenly distribute the weight gives the trimmers their name. The lowest of the engineering gang, they often socialize and eat separately from other crew members, as befits their existence at the bottom level of society and pay scale among the crew. Stokers shovel the coal into her ever-hungry seven boilers under the watchful eyes of the firemen who are tasked to keep the fires burning properly to produce the proper amounts of steam to drive the ship and her generators. Stewards, waiters, cooks, bakers, butchers, able and ordinary seamen, firemen, language interpreters, engineers, and electricians, and the one lone Marconi operator, all work with the ship's officers to keep this floating city operating to the Captain's standards. Always meticulous, Rostron keeps his keen eye on every detail. Even though it may only be another routine voyage with nothing of importance to note about this one specific Atlantic crossing, it will be done well and to the standards set by 'the Electric Spark'.

"You see Cecil; this is one of the older style Marconi sets. Just three years ago, there were only 125 ships in the mercantile marine with the Marconi apparatus. Now we have over 400 – it is almost universal in the Navy - and the newest ships get the newest equipment. But to me, it is the operator's duty to get the best out of what he has to work with. That is his job."

Dr. Blackmarr lounged behind the two young enthusiasts at Harold's small desk smoking a cigar listening to the lessons being taught.

"Our system is also located in many shore stations. Because they are on land, they can be large stations with great power. They help us relay messages that our smaller ship's Marconi isn't strong enough to send on its own. What I have here is the standard 1.5 kW set that has a range from 70 – 250 miles, but much more at night. This varies with conditions in the atmosphere that I can't completely explain, but even so, the range is much greater at night. The basics are this: I get my power from the ship's main electric system which converts it to the main terminals. This magnetic relay key opens and closes the path of the current. The different length and spacing of how I use the key is what sends the Morse code I showed you through the system and to the aerials. The aerials are those silicon bronze wires that stretch between the masts of the ship. I saw you looking at those on deck earlier. I commend you for trying to learn all you can."

"How fast can you send a message Mr. Cottam?"

"Well Cecil, I shouldn't brag but I was one of the fastest in my class at the Marconi school and have a very fast pace to this day. Each of us operators brag about different sending rates, but care needs to be taken to maintain the quality of the message. Too fast and the spark won't transmit properly, and the message ends up garbled and often then must be repeated."

Handing young Cecil a blank form titled 'The Marconi International Marine Communications Company Ltd.' Harold explains, "This is what I record the message on. I fill in the words as they are sent to me from shore or another ship. Or a passenger writes his or her message on the form. Usually, the purser figures out the charges to send it, and then I send their message to shore or another ship. See here? Let's fill it out…. our office of origin is the *Carpathia*, the date today is April 14, 1912, the office we are sending it to is – let's say – the RMS *Titanic*. We write MGY for the *Titanic*. Each ship has its own letters as an identifier instead of its name. Our sign is MPA."

"Let me show you some messages I have already taken so you can see what they are like. I have a few private messages I have sent for passengers already as well, but I cannot show you those."

From MSF (Caronia)

West bound steamers report Bergs, growlers and field ice 42° north and from 42° to 51° west. Regards Barr

From MBC (Baltic)

Captain Smith Titanic. Greek steamer Athenia reports passing icebergs and large quantities of field ice today in latitude 41° N, longitude 49° W

Wish you and Titanic all success. Commander

From DDR (Amerika)

Passed two large icebergs 41° north 50° west 14 April

"Now these were not directed to us but are general warnings. We will be well south of the areas mentioned. I know Dr. Blackmarr knows the Captain and I am sure he will show you our course and how we will sail safely past any of these warnings. Mr. Bisset can also show you. I have seen you with him a bit."

"He is teaching me and even let me help him last night. I stood right by him and called out, as four bells rang at 10:00, ALL'S WELL AND LIGHTS BURNING BRIGHTLY!"

"Well done, Cecil. You are turning into quite a seafaring young man."

"Indeed, he is. Now Cecil, we must go and prepare for dinner and let Mr. Cottam do his work."

The major daily highlight of any voyage experience is dinner at sea. While the *Carpathia* steams placidly along at 14 knots this April 14, 1912, the many cooks on the *Carpathia* prepare dinner for 734 passengers plus the officers and crew. Hot oysters Monaco, Ribs of beef, croquette potatoes and asparagus au

Bavarre fill Dr. Blackmarr's plate. Young – and less adventuresome - Cecil chooses instead Virginia ham and mashed potatoes. Only a few traces of the Victoria tartlettes desert remain when Dr. Blackmarr lights up his ever-present cigar. Sending Cecil to the cabin, a long stroll on the darkened deck ends the day. Glittering stars on an inky-black background do little to lighten the ship. Even the ship's lights seem to be absorbed by the blackness of the night. Dead calm. No ocean swell except where the water was disturbed by the movement of the ship. No wind. A brief flicker of Northern lights. Nothing else to be seen. Unbelievably still, water colder than the fresh water freezing temperature, and a sky darker than total blackness.

On *Titanic,* Peter Fletcher – the 26-year-old ship's bugler - has sounded both the call to dress and 'Roast Beef of Old England" call to dinner. The Hadnots go to the luxurious second-class dining saloon. Consommé of tapioca, curried chicken with rice, with American ice cream for dessert combine their tastes for both past and present. Elizabeth's mother eats little – as on previous nights – still consumed and brooding with worry about what will happen to her former charges at the orphanage. Her special worry is the little girls. She felt called to save as many as possible from life as Devadasis where girls as young as eight years are married to the Gods according to the Hindu custom; a life of service to the temple and sexual service to the men who visit the temples. She had fought the local villages and authorities and even been charged with kidnapping when caught taking a girl into the safety of the mission orphanage. She and her fellow female workers had dedicated themselves, and sometimes even forsaken marriage, to focus on the rescue, care, feeding, and education of the children. She could only pray and hope that the work would continue without her driving force. But family illness had forced her family to abandon their mission work in India and build a new life in America. As Mrs. Hadnot stares down at her full plate, she can only hope that the mission will continue to thrive and that they will find a welcome congregation in their new mission church in Ohio.

"Come, Mother Hadnot, you must cheer up and have some dinner. And you Elizabeth finish up your dinner as well. We will not find many curried dishes in Ohio. Do you really think you have eaten enough to get you through the night until morning?"

"All right Father. It is just that I hope I will like America. I have never been there, and it will be so different. Sometimes I think about it and worry."

"I understand. I am sure you will like it. After all, you are an American that is really your home. Now you can actually see it and live there, and you will have an entire farm to grow things, unlike the small area we had at the mission. Do not worry. Now, I hate to leave you ladies, but I must go to my discussion group now. A ship at sea makes for a captive audience, and probably the only way to get eight priests, ministers, and other missionaries with such different backgrounds, experiences, and outlooks to sit still and have a peaceful discussion. It is both rare and very stimulating for me. And yes Mother, I will report all salient points of interest when I join you later as always. I will get my long coat on the way. It is getting so bitterly cold out on deck."

"Thank you, Father. Don't be too late."

Walking the deck, even in the bitter cold, is a habit that helps center Reverend Hadnot and crystallizes his thoughts before going to his discussion group. Through a window, he catches a glimpse of the man representing the absolute apex of gilded age wealth, Colonel John Jacob Astor with his young wife Madeleine. The object of much envy and gossip due to his divorce and quick remarriage to such a young woman, Reverend Hadnot had found Colonel Astor to be the epitome of grace and politeness in the limited contacts they had made between the first and second classes on the ship. The Hadnot family had seen too much and experienced too much due to adherence to pure class distinction and rigid dogma of all kinds, including religion. He sometimes wondered if the caste system in India was any stricter than the class labels on polite society. Their faith had been forged by the heat of India and its deaths, illnesses, and the struggle to provide for orphans. Their conversions came about through work rather than words. Reverend Hadnot, and his wife, had little patience for the strict reliance on the forms of religion or society but instead built their lives on the visible, practical acts of faith. He knew that these thoughts were considered radical and blasphemous by a couple of the priests that were part of the discussion group, and they looked at him askance when he quietly tried to make his points. He was quite willing to accept Colonel Astor and his bride for the loving couple they showed themselves to be, whatever the circumstances. Forty-seven years old and divorced, Astor had discovered the seventeen-year-old ingénue while playing tennis in Bar Harbor, Maine. To be divorced, in particular, divorced only a couple of years, and to have a son older than his new bride created quite the scandal. The couple had taken an extended honeymoon in Europe to remove themselves from the gossip of the moneyed crowd in America. Deciding to return to New York when Madeleine began to demonstrate the symptoms of morning sickness, their party includes a manservant, maid, and nursemaid due to Madeleine's pregnancy occupies first-class cabins C62 and C45. The Astors are the undisputed pinnacle of the elite on board the ship. A life full of promise awaits them in their new marriage and the upcoming birth of their first child, and Hadnot wishes them nothing but peace and happiness.

Far below the still-fresh pine wood decking – deep in the bowels of the *Titanic* – trimmers had finally made progress in controlling the coal fire that had been burning long before she put to sea on her maiden voyage. Deep in one of her reserve coal bunkers – which had been only half full due to the coal strike in England – a long-smoldering fire had kept the trimmers busy since departure. Six hundred tons of coal had been moved from the bunker into her boilers and had allowed the extreme heat applied to the plates and rivets of her starboard side to subside. Coal fires and spontaneous combustion were a constant threat on the great coal-fired liners, and this fire had smoldered against the great lady's side plates, bulkheads, and rivets for weeks with unknown effect.

Far above Reverend Hadnot, lookouts Reginald Lee and Frederick Fleet assume the watch high up the mast in the frigid crow's nest. They talk of home, the cold, the smell of ice, and their request to Officers Wilde and Lightoller for binoculars to be kept in the crow's nest for the lookouts. While some lookouts and ship's officers dismiss the use of binoculars as actually reducing the lookout's ability to spot an object, the lookouts like to have a pair in the crow's next close at hand while at sea just in case. Second officer Blair had taken back the set he had lent to the lookouts for the first leg of the voyage. Now, no matter their preference, they would depend on their unaided eyesight in the biting wind of that cold night.

On the *Carpathia*, Harold hopes and plans to crawl into his bunk earlier than the last two nights. He is exhausted. Busy and awake until 3:00 a.m. the first night of the voyage and 2:30 a.m. last night had him yawning and stretching at his equipment table. Bisset has already come and gone. The Second Officer has started to come to the Marconi house to gossip about the ship's business and to watch and start to learn how the Marconi system works. He had left to take the 8:00 pm to midnight watch, after joking with Harold about the distance he had to walk from the aft boat deck where the Marconi shack was located up to the bridge.

"Cottam, I hope we never have a real emergency old man. You will run yourself ragged dashing up and down stairways and across almost the length of the ship to get to the wheelhouse. I hope you are fully fit and ready just in case. I joke with you, but I do hope you know that the Captain puts a lot of store in your work and the value of the wireless system. Well, I will leave you to finish your work so you can turn in before midnight tonight. I know you said you needed to do a time check and also want to monitor the land station for any news, especially about that bloody coal strike at home. Well, I will leave you to it, Mr. Cottam. I must say that when working from 7:00 a.m. until 3:00 a.m., you really earn your £ 4-10 per month."

Bisset's assurance about the new captain's belief in the value of Harold's work pleases him along with a feeling of pressure to be exact and accurate in all he did so as not to let Captain Rostron down. He had already made sure all the latest of today's ice warnings had been delivered to the bridge.

S.S. Mesaba reporting:

Extensive icefield 42° north to 49° west saw much heavy pack ice and great number large bergs and field ice

Weather good, clear.

S.S. Californian reporting:

We are stopped and surrounded by ice.

Captain Rostron is in the wheelhouse or one of the bridge wings constantly checking the sea conditions ahead. "Our course will take us far to the south of the reported ice, but it seems like a big field. We may have other ships steering south of the field which will require extra vigilance. Our Marconi man says we have the following within his range: the Norddeutscher Lloyd S.S. *Frankfort*; the Canadian Pacific S.S. *Mount Temple*; the Allan Liner S.S. *Virginian*; and a Russian cargo-steamer S.S. *Birma*, plus the *Mesaba, Baltic, Caronia, and the Californian*. So, between the bergs, growlers, and the ship traffic, it might get pretty crowded in our patch of sea. Oh, and of course, the *Titanic*. Everyone must keep a sharp lookout at all times. Carry on to your duties!"

The Captain walks back out to the port wing and stands quietly inspecting the sea conditions; calm weather, smooth sea, no wind, clear sky. There is no moon and the miracle of the Aurora Borealis is shimmering on the northern horizon.

"Mr. Bisset, this is a peculiar night. We have good visibility now. However, I believe the melting of the large ice field and the mixing of the Labrador Current and the Gulf Stream is going to make our work more difficult. See how the sea and the sky seem to blend into one another? It is very difficult to define the horizon clearly. And with the sea so calm, there won't be the usual breaking of waves on the base of any ice, so we must be very cautious."

Lapsing back into silence, Captain Rostron stands mutely gazing ahead at the sea and sky, and then raises his cap a few inches into his familiar prayer position and his lips move soundlessly for a few moments. Turning to leave the bridge wing, Rostron turns and speaks over his shoulder as he looks once more at the dark sea. "You may sight the *Titanic* if she bears southward to avoid the ice. I can't imagine Smith will try to run through it when the growlers and bergs are so thick that the *Californian* has stopped for the night. I know no growler can hurt us or the *Titanic*, but where growlers are prevalent, their bigger brother icebergs lurk. Are you sure the *Titanic* received the message Cottam copied about the *Californian* stopping for the night?"

"Yes sir. Cottam knows with certainty that *Titanic* received it. He told me that the *Californian* Marconi man was told to shut up since the operator on *Titanic* was busy sending messages and the *Californian*'s signal was interfering. Cottam told me that the *Californian* was shutting down for the night about 11:30 p.m. since they were stopped by the ice."

"Wireless is a wonderful thing, isn't it? I hear you have been spending time learning about the Marconi apparatus. Well done Bisset! Keep it up. Who knows when the need might arise to use it to its full capacity?"

"Thank you, sir. I am trying to learn."

Looking down at the black water from the wing one last time, Rostron murmurs softly to himself as much as Bisset, "We are in clear water here, but you must always keep your eyes sharp all the same because who knows what might be ahead. You know, I am actually sorry for Smith of the *Titanic*. That big beautiful new ship – carrying the expectations of all the newspaper clippings and with managing director Ismay on board – she is proving a slowcoach on her maiden voyage, and now this ice field will make him lose more time if he steers to the southward around it. I assume he will. She must be a wonderful ship, but all their bragging seems a kind of blasphemy, claiming she is unsinkable and all that kind of thing. Well, the night is clear, and I will turn in."

He returns to the large chart room, writes out his nightly standing orders, and leaves with a crisp "Goodnight."

Carpathia slowly goes to sleep, except for the constant quiet throb of her engines. No passengers are on deck on this frigid night, and the lights on deck and in the cabins go dark as the ship slumbers in the cold. Even Cottam is preparing to go to bed after trying one more time to get the news. Maybe just one more minute with the earphones on before shutting down will catch some tidbit of valuable news.

Elizabeth and her mother have given up waiting for the Reverend and turned into their bunks. The lights are off in *Titanic* cabin F4. Both sleeping - but not soundly. Nellie still has not found the peace and security that eludes her when on board a ship – especially when her husband isn't next to her - and Elizabeth is dreaming deeply about what Ohio might be like, and what was in store for her future.

"SIX BELLS – ALL IS WELL AND ALL LIGHTS BURNING BRIGHTLY."

Chapter Three

CALLING FOR HELP

Icebergs are an ancient creation. Near the time that Egyptian King Tutankhamen was having his tomb complex constructed in the dry dusty land west of the Nile River; another kind of construction is beginning nearly 7,000 miles away in the frigid wastes of western Greenland. Constant snowfall is accumulating and compressing into a material between snow and glacial ice called firn. Over ensuing decades, the firn compresses under the weight of the newer snowfalls into dense glacial ice. Slowly, patiently, the mass of ice moves towards the sea inch by inch. At the coast of the Arctic Ocean, tides and abuse from storms work persistently at the ice until sections – both large and small – calve from the glacier and crash into the sea. Centuries after the first moisture was deposited as snow, what is now called an iceberg floats in the Arctic Ocean at the mercy of storms, currents, and tides. The ice may appear white, blue where the air bubbles have been pressured out of the ice, or with streaks of green from the algae and other sea life thriving under the ice.

Traveling from Baffin Bay to the Davis Strait the growlers – small low-profile bergs the size of the *Titanic*'s grand piano and the large bergs – anywhere from 20-500 feet above the water - enter the Labrador Current. The vast majority of bergs will melt long before they can slowly make their way into the North Atlantic.

Only the largest and strongest can survive the warmer water temperature, and those that survive will only live two or three years in the waters of the Atlantic. Set in motion thousands of years in the past – and one of over 1,000 bergs that cross the 48° North latitude each year - a berg that may have started somewhere around 1,500 feet long and 300 feet tall, now glides on the saltwater currents of the North Atlantic on a moonless night in April 1912. Shrunken from its original size by wind and storm, it floats in quiet obscurity among many other bergs.

By 11:39 p.m. April 14, Cottam is preparing a list of the day's communications to take to the bridge of the *Carpathia* preparatory to shutting down for the night. His early entry into his bunk for the first time in three days is only minutes away. First Officer Dean is getting ready to assume the watch from James Bisset. The *Carpathia* is silent and dark, with only the whisper of the water being cut by her knife-like prow as she steams her way towards distant Gibraltar at 14 knots. On the giant *Titanic*, Frederick Fleet and Reginald Lee are staring into an unusual impenetrable haze ahead of the *Titanic* as she speeds along at 22.5 knots – just under her maximum speed. Captain EJ Smith has returned to the bridge after being the guest of honor at a gala dinner in the first-class dining saloon. He has been informed by Second Officer Lightoller of the new ice warnings and that the water temperature has dropped below the freezing mark of fresh water. The air temperature is also noted to have dropped to 33 degrees Fahrenheit. No moon, no wind, and a calm sea. Good conditions for a fast night run. He gives orders to be informed of any changes and retires to his cabin near the bridge. *Titanic's* Marconi room is still dispatching commercial traffic – called messages from millionaires by Harold Cottam on the *Carpathia*. Cottam's friend Jack Phillips is pushing to get his paying customer's messages transmitted from *Titanic* and get to bed himself. James Bisset is looking at the time and having thoughts of his warm bunk under *Carpathia's* bridge when First Officer Dean relieves him in a few minutes from the 8-12 watch. His Captain has retired to his cabin but is not yet fully asleep. Reverend Hadnot is just returning to his cabin to join his sleeping family, and while some *Titanic* passengers still wear their evening formal attire and socialize, most passengers on both liners are warmly slumbering in their cabins. Less than a minute ahead - hidden in the haze - floating silently on the frigid water is an altered or extinguished future for thousands of people this April night.

"ICEBERG RIGHT AHEAD!" Crow's nest lookout Fleet screams into the phone after ringing the *Titanic*'s bell three times signaling something directly ahead in the ship's path. Then he and fellow lookout Lee can do nothing but watch the looming shape come into clearer view out of the haze and strangely altered horizon just off the starboard bow as the *Titanic* labors to turn. The great ship vibrates as she desperately tries to turn hard-a-starboard and reverse her powerful engines. "No. We should keep the speed up to swing her around the berg. Don't slow her down! Remember, the biggest part of the berg is what we can't see. That part is underwater, and we need to swing well around. Turn your beautiful bastard, turn!" Only seconds later, both lookouts think they might miss as the ship begins to respond to the threat, but the berg scrapes down the starboard side of the ship with a grinding sound leaving sheared ice on the forward well deck and the two lookouts aghast and staring at each other. "I think we might have missed the worst of it though."

She did not miss; not with 7/8 of the berg hidden under the water. The Atlantic Ocean cascades into the new ship filling the forepeak tank and the first, second, and third holds. The fifth and sixth boiler rooms will soon be flooded as well. The massive liner is drifting to a stop, wounded and in pain. First-class passengers in the highest deck cabins on the ship barely notice the slight shudder; the lowest class feel the collision the most. A screeching, grinding sound reverberates through the lower levels of the starboard side cabins and holds. Captain EJ Smith, his instincts honed by over forty years at sea, gets to the bridge immediately.

"What have we struck Mr. Murdoch?"

"We have struck an iceberg. I put her hard-a-starboard and ran the engines full astern, but it was too close; she hit it."

Being on her maiden voyage, *Titanic* has the services of her designer Andrews, the managing director of the line Ismay, and the cream of the crop of Harland & Wolff's technical engineers in person. All the accumulated wisdom and experience of these on board including the ship's builder, designer, line director, and their most experienced Captain conclude that their skills and knowledge are of no use. With more of her watertight compartments opened to the frigid waters than any designer anticipated, there's nothing to be done. The automatic doors to close off the compartments have been electrically closed from the bridge but are unable to isolate the flow. It is too much for the pumps to handle. As each compartment fills, the water is spilling over into the next compartment aft as the bulkheads have not been constructed all the way up to the deckheads. The order has already been given to close the dampers to reduce the fires in the boilers and vent steam to lessen the danger of an explosion. The super liner is doomed. She is already settling down by the head. Now it is only a question of time.

"Prepare the lifeboats. Mr. Boxhall, please confirm our exact position. I have done a rough calculation and am taking it myself to the wireless room to save time."

"Is it really serious Captain?"

"Mr. Andrews tells me he gives her an hour to an hour and a half."

Fourth Officer Boxhall retreats to the chart room to calculate the exact position of *Titanic* and submits the position to the Captain on his return. The position update is taken to the Marconi room.

When the Captain first bursts in, Harold Bride is still laboring to finish the backload of their commercial messages that had piled up due to the Marconi system being out of service the previous day. Jack Phillips is finally off duty and has turned the earphones over to Bride as he gets ready for bed when the Captain comes into the Marconi room.

"You had better get assistance." When Mr. Phillips hears the Captain's calm voice he comes out and asks him if he wants him to use a distress call. He said, "Yes; at once." Phillips immediately takes back the key and prepares to send the distress signal – along with *Titanic*'s three-letter call sign - with the ship's position.

CQD CQD CQD CQD CQD CQD MGY MGY MGY MGY

REQUIRE IMMEDIATE ASSISTANCE. COME AT ONCE.

WE STRUCK AN ICEBERG. SINKING.

LAT. 41.46 N., LONG. 50.24 W.

(12:17 a.m.)

On *Carpathia*, the day is ending. For a very few minutes just after midnight, Harold Cottam is away from the wireless set and in the wheelhouse turning over his summary of all the day's Marconigrams and ice warnings received to First Officer Dean. One more long trek back to the Marconi shack and then an early night for the first time on this voyage. He had left the wireless operating intending to make one more attempt to confirm his time check with the *Parisian* when he returns before shutting down for the night. His bunk beckons. He dons the earphones again which are an almost permanent part of his anatomy for the last time of his long day. Harold takes off his coat and begins to change out of his Marconi uniform for bed. Knowing that *Titanic* is close and being aware of the flood of messages being sent to her from Cape Cod, Harold contacts his friend Jack Phillips on *Titanic* to see if he can accept the messages Harold has already taken for forwarding to Phillips and Bride on *Titanic*. One quick favor for a friend and then off to sleep.

MPA CALLING MGY

(Carpathia calling Titanic – 12:21 a.m.)

K

(Go ahead)

G M O M

(Good morning old man)

I say old man, do you know there is a batch of messages coming through for you from MCC? (Cape Cod)

CQD CQD SOS SOS CQD SOS

Come at once, We have stuck a berg. CQD OM.

Position 41.46 N., 50.14 W.

CQD SOS

It is 12:22 a.m., April 15, 1912. *Titanic* sends out distress messages to any and all ships within range of her powerful transmitter. The wireless screams for help are coming fast and furious to anyone within range of her transmitter.

MPA from MGY

(Carpathia from Titanic 12:25 a.m.)

CQD CQD

MGY from MPA

(Titanic from Carpathia)

Shall I tell my Captain? Do you require assistance?

MPA from MGY

(Carpathia from Titanic)

Yes, come quick!

Here corrected position 41.46 N., 50.14 W. Require immediate assistance. We have collided with iceberg. Sinking. Can nothing hear for noise of steam.

(Sent about 15 to 20 times)

Pausing only long enough to put his uniform coat back on, Harold pounds down the stairs from the Marconi house on the raised boat deck and heads towards the bow. Dashing unseeing past the second class dining saloon, past the funnel, he reaches the stairs to the wheelhouse, and his feet ring on the metal steps. Harold's normal calm reserve is gone when he skids to a stop in front of First Officer Dean and hands him the crumpled message form.

"And Mr. Cottam where is your uniform cap? You know how the Captain is about things like that."

"Read it! The *Titanic* has hit a berg and is in distress!"

"Are you serious? Have you confirmed this? I think you should check it again. It might be a mistake or a prank. This is, after all, the *Titanic* we are talking about."

"I know it is the *Titanic*. I know those two boys on the *Titanic*. They are both friends of mine and this is no prank or mistake. I'll go directly to the Captain then and you can just bugger off." Cottam's unusual outburst and passion immediately convince Dean of the seriousness and he moves to follow the young Marconi man to the Captain's cabin. Dean and Cottam clatter down the stairs and burst in on the Captain with breathless apologies at 12:35 a.m., waking Rostron from his semi-slumber with their unexpected entrance.

"Captain, CQD from *Titanic*. She has struck a berg and is asking for assistance."

"Mr. Dean, turn the ship. Bend on all speed and head North-West. I shall be there presently with an exact course."

"Aye, sir."

"Are you sure Mr. Cottam? Are you quite sure?"

"Yes sir."

"Well then, send to *Titanic* that we are turning around and steaming full force towards you. I will be on the bridge, so immediately bring me any updates as you receive them. I will need your utmost attention as to what is transpiring so I can act accordingly."

"Aye, sir. I will return to my equipment."

Rostron finds the *Carpathia*'s current position and works out a course towards the *Titanic*. He summons his Chief Engineer as he dresses. Emerging on the bridge, Rostron crisply orders "North 52 West – 308 degrees true - Full ahead!" 58 miles to go if the position given is correct. The maximum speed of RMS *Carpathia* 14 knots. One of the junior officers is sent to inform Harold to tell *Titanic* they would reach the stated position in about four hours. Four hours. "Tell Engineer Johnstone I need to see him and the rest of my officers in the chart room immediately."

MGY from MPA

(12:32 a.m.)

We are putting about and heading for you.

"Mr. Johnstone, I need the best efforts of your entire engineering department. At our normal cruising speed, we will require four hours and ten minutes to reach the position given by *Titanic*. Order another watch of stokers turned to. All stokers and trimmers are to report for duty immediately. Divert the steam from the ship's heating and hot water systems into her engines. Bend on every ounce of steam and every knot of speed she has in her. Come back and report progress to me." Turning to the rest of the now assembled officers he quickly outlines the situation. "Gentleman the *Titanic* has stuck a berg and is in distress fifty-eight miles from here on the bearing N. 52W. We will make our utmost speed in going to her rescue. Doctor McGee, Purser Brown, Chief Steward Hughes here are my orders."

1. English doctor with assistants to remain in the first-class dining room
2. Italian doctor with assistants to remain in second class dining room
3. Hungarian doctor with assistants remain in third class dining room
4. Each doctor to have supplies of restoratives, stimulants, and everything on hand for immediate needs of probably wounded or sick

5. Purser, with the assistant and chief stewards to receive passengers, etc., at gangways, with our own steward in assisting Titanic passengers to the dining rooms, also to get Christian and surnames of all survivors as soon as possible to send by wireless
6. Inspector, steerages stewards, and master at arms to control our own steerage passengers and keep them out of the third-class dining hall and out of the way and off the deck to prevent confusion
7. Chief steward to have all hands to have coffee, etc read to serve out to all our crew
8. Have coffee, tea, soup, etc., in each saloon, blankets in saloons, at the gangways, and some for our lifeboats
9. See all rescued cared for and immediate wants attended to
10. My cabin and all officers' cabins to be given up. Smoke rooms, library, dining rooms, would be utilized to accommodate the survivors
11. All spare berths in steerage to be utilized for Titanic passengers and get all our own steerage passengers grouped together
12. Stewards to be placed in each alleyway to reassure our own passengers should they enquire about noise in getting our boats out or the working of engines
13. To all, I strictly remind you of the necessity for order, discipline, and quietness to avoid all confusion.

Climbing to the bridge, Rostron can feel the surge of power under his feet as the *Carpathia* responds to the call for her best efforts and highest speed.

MGY to MPA

SOS Titanic. We are sinking. About all down. Sinking...

(12:40 a.m.)

"Chief Officer Hankinson, and Officer Dean, here are my orders for the deck officers and crew."

1. Chief and first officer: All hands to be called out, get coffee, etc.
2. Prepare and swing out all our boats
3. All gangway doors to be opened
4. Electric light sprays in each gangway and overside
5. A block with line rove hooded in each gangway
6. A chair sling at each gangway for getting up sick or wounded
7. Boatswains' chairs, pilot ladder, and canvas bags for lifting children
8. Cargo falls with both ends clear, bowlines in the ends, and bights secured along ship's sides for boat ropes or to help people up
9. Heaving lines distributed along the ship's side and gaskets handy near gangways for lashing people in chairs
10. Forward derricks, topped and rigged, and steam on winches
11. Each of you knows your own particular duties for your station in addition to this
12. Company's rockets to be fired at 2:45 a.m. and every quarter-hour after to reassure Titanic
13. Pour oil down forwards lavatories on both sides of the ship in case it is necessary to calm the sea on arrival
14. Each officer to report to me personally on the bridge that all my orders are carried out and that everything is in readiness

"Mr. Bisset, I need you for a special duty."

"Sir?"

"You are well known for your exceptional eyesight. Station yourself on the starboard bridge wing. Keep a keen eye for lights, flares, and especially ice. I have placed extra lookouts in the crow's nest, on the bow, and the port bridge wing, but I going to principally depend on you here. We are driving our ship all out into danger and I need every ounce of effort and concentration to help us in our mission and keep our passengers safe. Mr. Cottam says no one can raise the *Californian*, even though she is much closer to the *Titanic* than we. The other ships he is receiving are all more distant. The *Virginian* – 170 miles, the *Baltic* – 243 miles, the *Frankfurt* – 140 miles, and the *Olympic* is over 500 miles. That is a lot of assistance to be sure, but we cannot chance to wait on anyone. We must assume the worst and plan as if we are the only ship in the North Atlantic tonight." Once again Rostron lifts his cap and murmurs a quick prayer before fixing Bisset with a stern look.

"Aye, sir."

Just after the stroke of midnight on the Titanic, Reverend Hadnot is hurrying back to his family. Seeing light under the cabin door, Reverend Hadnot steps confidently into the cabin to find both his daughter and wife awake and alert. Still in his formal evening dress – erect and grand - his composed face and manner project calm confidence for his ladies.

"Hello, my ladies! I see you are awake. There's talk that the ship has bumped an iceberg."

Roughly twenty minutes earlier, Elizabeth had woken when a shudder ran through the cabin causing a rattling in the room and the clinking of glasses together on the washstand. Elizabeth had turned on her bunk light and leaned over the edge of the top bunk to look at her mother as she turned her light on as well. Mrs. Hadnot looked at her daughter with wide eyes, her desire to project a parent's composure being overwhelmed by her instinctive fear of the sea.

"Let me try to see what happened, mother."

Bounding down the small wooden ladder from her bunk, she crosses the cabin and unclips the porthole, and looks out, giving a short gasp as the frigid wind hits her face. As her eyes adjust, she can see the ship's lights reflected in the water and the churning water at the stern as the propellers desperately thrash the dark water. By the time her mother looks out only a moment later, both the sea and the ship's constant engine noises have fallen silent.

"I believe we have stopped Elizabeth. I wonder what could be happening. Now let's close this window before we both catch our death."

"Elizabeth – Nellie – best to get dressed warmly while we sort out what has happened. I am sure there is nothing to worry about, but as we have always done at the mission, let us be prepared for any eventuality. I will find a steward and try to learn more and be back with you shortly. Now, not to worry, but best get dressed and I will return." Pausing before leaving the cabin, Hadnot reaches the top of the clothing wardrobe and pulls down two life jackets. "Hold on to these. I am sure they won't be needed but keep them close and I will be right back."

Elizabeth sits close to her mother on the lower bunk to get and give comfort. Nellie sits wide-eyed and motionless.

"Come mother. Let us do as father said. I will help." Dressed in layers of their warmest clothes including long serge topcoats, Nellie and Elizabeth sit red-faced and overheated until Reverend Hadnot returns.

"Come. We have been instructed to go up on deck. I am sure it will be all right though."

"WHAT?'

"Come, dear. Let us follow instructions. It will be fine, I am sure. Let me help you with these life jackets. They can be cumbersome and a bit hard to handle."

"Father, why aren't you putting on a life jacket as well?"

"Not to worry my love. I will get you and your mother sorted out and then get myself ready. I am sure there is nothing to worry about and you will be tucked back in your bunk after a bit. I see others already returning to their cabins to go back to bed. But let us make sure."

Making their way with only a few others down the long passageway, the Hadnot family climbs the stairs to the Second-Class Promenade Deck. Continuing up the stairs, they pass several passengers descending complaining about the cold on deck and grumbling they were going back to bed and get a good night's sleep. Reverend Hadnot has long since decided which lifeboat would be his target if any worst-case scenario would arise during the voyage. He and his small family find their way there and join a group already gathered. Below where he stands on the boat deck, he can barely hear the *Titanic* orchestra playing lively tunes over the sound of the venting steam. There is much confusion and many rumors as they stand in the biting wind.

"Well Allen, no one seems overly worried about this, even with that infernal noise. Maybe I can relax then."

"I am sure dear. Still, we will wait here just in case it is needed to get into that lifeboat they are uncovering and float around for a short time. It still seems like this is not too much to worry about, but I have heard every rumor from having no real damage and we will be back in our warm beds in no time, to having to return to England for repairs. So, we will wait and see."

"I am Fifth Officer Lowe. I am the ship's officer in charge of this station and am here to assist you and ensure your safety. We will load the boats now! We need to load right smartly. So let us get a bloody move on!"

The Hadnots have been standing far back from the side of the ship stamping their feet and clutching their arms to keep warm. Only now as they approach the side do they realize how the great ship is already angled down at the bow and is tilting down to one side. Elizabeth thinks about asking her father whether it is to port or starboard, as she could never remember which side was which but thought better of the question. The ship is seriously wounded and in distress. Deep distress. She is going down. This is not just an exercise.

"Come, my ladies, it is time for you to load the boat."

"But father. What about you? There aren't that many boats."

"Well, you see my child; the lifeboats on a ship like this aren't designed to hold every single passenger at once. That is why there aren't more boats. They are designed to ferry people to other ships in case of trouble. I am sure that will happen. If I can't get in the next boat, I will simply wait for one to return after another ship arrives and picks you up. I am sure it will be ok. I just need to wait my turn."

Trying to make himself heard over the roar of the super heated steam being vented above them is difficult. Only the shouts of the lifeboat officers rise above the din.

Elizabeth gives her father a hard hug. He holds her tighter than even when he saved her in her swimming accident back at the mission. She looks at him with questioning eyes and he smiles gently at her. Husband and wife told tight to each other as Elizabeth is assisted by a crewman into the boat. Nellie caresses Allen's cheek with her fingertips before resting her hand against his face before parting. Leaving him and seated next to her daughter, Nellie looks only at her husband, the center of her life and a great and good man.

"I love you, Allen."

"Now don't worry my loves, I will see you both in New York."

MPA to MGY

We are coming as quickly as possible and expect to be there within four hours.

MGY to MPA

T U O M (Thank you old man)

(12:45 a.m.)

On *Carpathia*, all the officers are on alert as she charges into a known ice field at her top speed. Johnstone is forcing everything he can out of her flaming boilers and pouring it into steam for the pounding engines. As the speed approaches *Carpathia*'s maximum effort the Chief Engineer quietly drapes his cap over the steam pressure gauge near the boilers so it can't be seen by his engineering crew. All storerooms are being quickly ransacked for blankets, brandy, medicines, and bandages. The dining tables are prepared to feed the *Titanic* passengers. With well over 2,000 of *Titanic*'s passengers and crew added to the *Carpathia*'s current compliment, every inch of the ship will be used and every provision needed for the over 3,000 people to fill every inch of the ship. Coffee for 1,000 is being brewed.

MGY to MKC

(RMS Olympic)

(1:25 a.m.)

We are putting the women off in boats.

"LOWER AWAY!"

Officer Lowe checks his pocket watch and notes the time of 1:25 a.m. as the lifeboat is slowly lowered towards the still black sea below. Fearing panicked leaps into the loaded boat from lower decks, he fires his revolver once each time as the boat passes A, B, and C decks as a warning. Crewmen play out the ropes above and the lifeboat descends ever so slowly. Five minutes – ten minutes – forever to the frightened passengers. Suddenly the stern of the boat stops lowering about five feet from the water. Was it a simple malfunction? Has panic on the deck above overwhelmed the lowering crew? No way to tell from down close to the sea surface. No option left so the ropes are let loose and the passengers scream as the 30-foot-long Clinker-built crashes down into the water. With the boat hopefully unharmed, the passengers reseat themselves and make sure there are no injuries. Nellie Hadnot is paralyzed with fright and even the bravery of youth is starting to wane for Elizabeth. The sight of her father silhouetted in the ship's brightly burning lights far above them, as he lights a cigar, tears into her. He gives a slow wave to his family as her tears start. There is a great silence in the boat. A mixed group of 1st, 2nd, and 3rd class passengers – mostly women and children – fill most of the boat. One passenger – a man – looks furtively out from under the woman's shawl he has used to evade the women and children directive from the loading officers. No one looks at him or speaks to him. No one speaks at all. The sounds from the ship – screams, wrenching metal, and the ever-present orchestra music now that the venting has stopped – float out from 150 yards away. At uneven intervals, a rocket soars into the sky from the *Titanic* as she sinks lower and lower. Somewhere behind her Elizabeth hears a man's voice say, "Why are they firing the rockets that way? Sending them up at random times means that the ship is having navigational problems and to stay out of the way. They need to send them up one every minute like clockwork to signal distress!" Elizabeth can barely see but can make out the appearance of a White Star uniform but does not recognize the man. She turns back and tries to find her father on the slanting deck of *Titanic*. The other lifeboat passengers stare in horrified fascination at the dying liner looming up against the starry sky. Several inches of icy water swirl under the feet of the passengers – possibly impact damage as it was dropped. No one speaks to anyone else. No introductions are made. Just the screams of those still on the ship and in the water and the orchestra music fill the air. Their music has changed from the jaunty airs played earlier to musically tell people that all is well. More somber – more religious – more soothing music now floats out over the water as the ship descends in the dark.

From MGY

(1:35 a.m.)

We are putting passengers off in small boats. Weather calm.

Engine room getting flooded.

MGY to MPA

(1:45 a.m.)

Come as quickly as possible. Engine room filing up to the boilers.

Cannot last much longer. Losing power.

T U O M G N

(Thank you old man good night)

RMS *Carpathia* is doing her best to meet the moment. She is shuddering and vibrating as she channels every ounce of her power into every knot of speed she could give. Engineer Johnstone reports to the bridge at 1:30 a.m. that everything that can possibly be done is being done. Her passengers are starting to awaken to a feeling that something unusual was happening. Within the ship, the pounding feet on the stairs and decks had awakened many. While Captain Rostron has instructed the stewards to ask the first- and second-class passengers firmly but politely to go back to their cabins, as the word spreads, more and more passengers learn of the true nature of the events of this night and make their way out onto the cold decks. 'Did you hear? – It can't be – All the running feet and the whistle woke us – They told me to go back to my cabin – The first steward told me he was not at liberty to say what was happening' runs the litany of comments from the gathered passengers. Each officer and doctor reports to the Captain that his orders have been carried out and all is in readiness for whatever will be found. The extra crow's nest and bow lookouts stare face-on into the cold seeking the slightest danger. *Carpathia* plunges on through the inky-black night at her maximum possible speed directly towards a killing ice field.

No more wireless messages reach the *Carpathia,* but the air is filled with questions and concern. Silence reigns from the *Californian* just a few miles from *Titanic*. She sits motionless and completely silent. No response from rockets, messages, or signal light. Nothing.

Virginian hears Titanic calling very faintly with reduced power – no response

Virginian hears Titanic call CQ but signal ends abruptly

Cape Race – We have not heard from Titanic for about half an hour.

Mount Temple hears Frankfurt calling Titanic with no response

Carpathia calls Titanic repeatedly with no response

Aboard lifeboat 14 they have experienced the completely unexpected and unbelievable. *Titanic* is gone. The magnificent liner, such a short time ago filled with light and life has died and slid out of sight about 2:20 a.m. after her two-hour and forty-minute struggle against an inevitable fate. The sounds of her death will never leave those that survive this night. Explosions within the great ship, the sound of the huge funnels crashing into the sea and onto swimmers in the water. The cracking sound as her strong spine splits and breaks. The muffled rumbling sounds of underwater explosions as the deep swallows the last life of the mega-ship as a last goodbye. Her passengers that could not find a place in one of the few lifeboats have a much shorter struggle ahead of them, only minutes. The piercing pain of the intensely cold water makes them cry out and – with the ship's noisy death struggle gone - the sounds of screams fill the night. Screams of those left on the decks of the sinking ship until the last moment and now thrust into the sea. Weaker screams of those who had jumped earlier into the below-freezing water. Screams of those looking for husbands, sons, daughters, and wives in the water. Screams for help towards the distant lifeboats – some boats only half- full. Screams that would live on for a lifetime in the minds of the survivors. Nellie and Elizabeth shiver in the cold. They shiver knowing Allen Hadnot is gone from them forever. They shiver under the weight of the screams – and then under the silence as the screams diminish and fade away as the swimmers freeze and die. Most of the youngest and healthiest last up to about fifteen minutes in the 28-31° water. The older and more infirm people in the water survive only moments. Elizabeth replays in her mind over and over her father's question to her about whether she had had enough food at her final meal on the *Titanic* to last her. Was it her last meal?

Officer Lowe transfers some of the passengers to other lifeboats so 14 can return to look for any survivors now that the people in the water had 'quieted down' and the threat of the boat being swamped by panicky swimmers has passed. Nellie refuses to be moved. She will stay anchored to this seat in this boat no matter what happens. She refuses to look up as 14 makes its way slowly through the floating bodies to find a few survivors which they pull into the boat. She stares in horror at the first person pulled aboard the lifeboat. He is too far gone and dies shortly after being rescued. His body –with its blue skin and icy hair - lies at her feet. Elizabeth pulls herself up against her mother and wraps herself in her mother's blanket after using her own to cover the body from her mother's sight.

MPA calling MGY

If you are there, we are firing rockets. We are rushing to you.

"Fire signal rockets every fifteen minutes and follow by our Cunard Roman candles."

"Aye Captain. They will play with the vision of our lookouts."

"I know. However, we have no choice. We must give those people hope and let them know we are coming."

"Aye, sir."

2:45 a.m. - *Carpathia* spots her first iceberg. A reflection of starlight off an indistinct shape attracts the eagle-eyes of Bisset on the wing. Rostron turns the ship to starboard and reduces speed to one- half and the old immigrant trade ship deftly dances around her first threat. Rostron personally moves the engine command back to full speed and *Carpathia* surges ahead once more. Now begins the time of threat and stress. *Carpathia* zigzags among bergs of all sizes. Small growlers grind along her hull plates as the passengers on deck stare down in worry at the sea. Small bursts of speed and quick course changes follow hard on one another in the dangerous seas as they approach *Titanic*'s last known position.

"I SEE A LIGHT. NOT A LINE OF LIGHTS, BUT A SINGLE LIGHT! AND NOW THERE IS A ROCKET"

One of the lifeboats has been firing green signals periodically in hopes of someone – anyone – seeing the boat. Now there is both an answering rocket and a distinct light in the distance. The same unknown sailor behind Elizabeth tells her that a single light instead of a line of lights means that whatever ship is coming is heading directly for them. Help has almost arrived. No one on the lifeboat knows for sure, but it is about 3:30 a.m.

Carpathia slows and then stops her engines. The silence on board her decks is deafening. All eyes watch. She has made the expected four-hour trip in three and one-half hours. Now she searches with a hopeful heart for another signal. There! Low on the horizon, it cannot be the masthead light of the giant liner *Titanic*. It is too low in the sky. Moving carefully, she approaches only to have to dodge once more around a twenty-foot-high iceberg. "Hard over! Full astern!" Only then does a mast appear and then the lifeboat below it. A ship's officer stands in the stern calling through cupped hands.

"I can't handle the lifeboat very well. We have women and children and only one seaman down here!"

"Mr. Bisset. Go overside with two assistants and board her as she comes alongside. Fend her off so that she doesn't bump and be careful that she doesn't capsize." A chop has come up on the ocean with the approaching dawn and some of the passengers are sick from the sudden motion of the boat. All are numbed with cold and sadness. The Jacob's ladder, bosun's chairs, and even ash bags for the children are lowered and then the passengers are hauled upwards to safety. The last to leave the first rescued lifeboat is James Boxhall, the Fourth Officer of the now-former *Titanic*. He is taken to the bridge.

"I am Captain Rostron. Welcome to *Carpathia*. Where is *Titanic*?"

"Captain, I am Fourth Officer Boxhall. She is gone, sir. Sank at 2:20 a.m. She was hoodoo'd from the beginning…There were sixteen boats and four collapsibles. Women and children were ordered into the boats…the boats were launched from 12:45 onwards…my boat was cleared away at 1:45 a.m.… many of the boats were only half-full…people wouldn't go into them…they didn't believe she would sink…. hundreds and hundreds were left on board…maybe a thousand…some even went back to bed…. good God sir…. I fired flares…. they couldn't live in this cold water…. we had room for a dozen in my boat…. the other boats must be near…"

"Easy now son. Easy now. Go below now lad and get some coffee and try to get warm."

As the dawn breaks, the view from the bridge shows dozens of icebergs; among them four or five big bergs up to two hundred feet above the waterline and dozens of smaller growlers all around. To the north a field of pack ice, a small patch of debris, and scattered within sight other lifeboats feebly rowing trying to make their way towards *Carpathia*. Dr. Blackmarr and young Cecil line the rails with other passengers pointing out lifeboats as they appear pulling slowly through the remnants of deck chairs, silk-covered couches, pillows, and other personal items and vast quantities of floating cork. Harold Cottam has woken his new friend on one of the many trips between his Marconi equipment and the bridge and Blackmarr has been watching each new development since before dawn. He murmurs to himself about the lack of debris and his scientific mind wonders why there aren't bodies visible. Such speculations can't be made aloud. Nothing breaks the ghastly silence of the rescued and the rescuers. He bows his head as a woman's hat floats by followed by a fur coat suspended from a piece of polished mahogany – now wreckage floating over a grave.

"EIGHT BELLS – ALL IS WELL - ALL LIGHTS BURNING BRIGHTLY"

Chapter Four

CONSEQUENTIAL ACTS

Everyone has their own story. Eyewitnesses to great events and wrenching disasters absorb and process events very differently. Great heroism and abject cowardice exist side by side. Modest acts of humanity and scandalous performances happen by turns. Reputations are enhanced or ruined in an instant. The long night of April 14-15, 1912 was just such an event. And disaster

The iceberg that opened *Titanic*'s starboard side to the Atlantic Ocean at 11:40 p.m. was a white wall looming up out of the sea over 200 feet high. Or it was a low floating berg hardly of a size of consequence. Passengers were blinded by the close presence of a sheet of ice directly out their porthole when they went to discover what was happening. Or there was no ice in sight anywhere. Utter calmness was reported throughout the sinking along with panicked passengers rushing the loading officers with shots fired. All actions witnessed by passengers with absolute confidence in the accuracy of the reports. Thirteen witnesses swore that the great ship broke in two before sinking, while four – including the surviving *Titanic* officers – testified that she went to her grave in one piece. J. Bruce Ismay handled himself with bravery and concern for his passengers while helping to load several lifeboats, while others maintain he cravenly snuck into a lifeboat to save his own life. Many of the surviving men are under a lifetime sentence of gossip – accused of sneaking into the boats dressed as women. Even the final song played by the *Titanic* musicians is reported differently by different witnesses. Was it the hymn that band leader Hartley had said in the past he would play if in that situation? The one that was normally played at funerals of the musicians union? Or was it one totally different as reported by the second Marconi operator? No facet of the disaster is more open to debate - and none has more differing interpretations and more long-lasting effects on survivors' lives - than the terrifying sounds, words, and actions in the lifeboats.

Lifeboat 7 is the first to be launched by Mr. Murdoch. She is put in the water with only 28 aboard, far under her capacity of 65. Some of the ship's officers maintain that the boat will collapse if lowered fully loaded. The lifeboat drill for earlier that Sunday had been canceled by Captain Smith. Instructions are given to pick up more passengers from the lower doors of the ship or in the water. No one is picked up. Occupants like silent film star Dorothy Gibson – who will star in a *Titanic* movie only one month after the sinking - and Margaret Hays with her Pomeranian Bebe, first stem the leaking in the boat caused by a missing plug with various bits of clothing and then shout down lookout Hogg who attempts to return to pick up floundering swimmers.

Lifeboat 5 – In the charge of Third Officer Herbert Pitman – is one of several boats having difficulty being lowered due to poor training and possibly the freshness of the ropes and pulleys. Bruce Ismay assists in the loading of the boat. Occupants like Karl Behr, the American tennis star, and Annie Stengel – who is knocked unconscious and breaks two ribs when passenger Dr. Frauenthal jumps into the boat to save himself while it is being lowered – are among the 38 passengers loaded. They saddle Pitman with guilt when he gives in to their protestations against going back for others. "Why should we lose all our lives in a useless attempt to save others?" No attempt is made.

Lifeboat 3 rows away from Titanic with 39 people on this frigid night. Henry Harper, the publisher, with his wife and Egyptian interpreter Hammad Hassab their Pekinese dog Sun Yat Sen, Edith Graham, wife of William Graham the founder of the Dixie Cup Company, also experience the fear-inducing stops and starts of the difficult lowering process. They too do not return to pickup those in the water but spend the time after the sinking bickering amongst the woman passengers over the annoyances of the night. Heiress Charlotte Cardeza sits with her son and two servants ruminating about the 14 trunks of clothes, 4 suitcases, 3 crates of baggage, her 6 - 7/8 carat pink diamond ring, and over 90 pairs of gloves now on the bottom of the sea.

Lifeboat 8 leaves the *Titanic,* with only 28 people, under the command of able-bodied seaman Thomas Jones. It contains the widows of the founder of Bucknell University and the industrialist George Wick. The Countess of Rothes takes control of the tiller and helps row and is called 'more of a man that any we had aboard'. Also on board is Ellen Bird, the maid of Ida, and Isidor Straus, the co-owner of Macy's department store. Ida had refused to enter the boat with her maid when her husband was told he could not enter the boat and said, 'I do not wish any distinction in my favor which is not granted to others.' His wife of 40 years refused to enter the boat. 'I will not be separated from my husband. As we have lived, so will we die – together.' In contrast, one female passenger is incensed and complains constantly about the stewards in the boat smoking as they wait for rescue in the half-empty boat.

Lifeboat 1 is lowered into the dark sea at 1:05 a.m. and leaves the ship with only 12 occupants. Twelve. The most famous occupants – Sir Cosmo Duff-Gordon and his wife Lucy – are two of the five first-class passengers along with seven crewmen occupying the boat. With a capacity of 40, the boat does not return to pick up anyone. The boat's occupants all stoutly deny hearing any mention of the idea of attempting to rescue any of the freezing swimmers. Duff-Gordon offers each crew member five pounds. He says it is to help them start again since they have lost everything in the sinking. Others say it was a bribe to prevent the crew from going back and risking their lives. Nothing can be proved in either direction, but he lives with the consequences of offering those crewmen 'a fiver' for the rest of his life.

Lookout Frederick Fleet and Quartermaster Hichens commands Lifeboat 6, which launches within minutes of boat 1. Margaret Brown wasn't planning on entering this boat. However, a crewman picks her up bodily and drops her into the boat as it is being lowered. Quartermaster Hichens refuses to row or to allow the boat to return. 'There's no use going back. There are only a lot of stiffs out there. It is our lives now, not theirs.' When Hichens tells the rowers to stop rowing to prevent an attempted return, Margaret Brown threatens to throw him overboard and starts the ladies rowing, including the beautiful socialite Helen Churchill Candee. Hichens will later dispute all accusations. Boat six had space for 38 more people.

Millionaire Benjamin Guggenheim assists his French mistress Leontine Pauline Aubart into lifeboat 9 before it lowers away about 1:30. He and his valet then remove their life jackets and fully dressed in formal evening attire, tell a steward 'We've dressed in our best, and are prepared to go down like gentlemen. Tell my wife I played the game out straight and to the end. No women shall be left aboard this ship because Ben Guggenheim was a coward.' Fifty-six occupants sit shivering as it rows away from Titanic in #9.

Lifeboat 2 is lowered from the port side after a large group of men who had already swarmed into the boat are ordered out by Second Officer Lightoller threatening them with an unloaded revolver. 'Get out of there you damned cowards! I'd like to see every one of you overboard!' Seventeen occupants spaced themselves around boat 2 and refuse to row the boat back to attempt to save the drowning. An emergency cutter with a capacity of 40, it rows away with more than twenty-three empty seats.

The last of the wooden lifeboats to be launched is lifeboat #4. Instructed to be lowered from the Promenade deck instead of the boat deck by Captain Smith himself, the Captain may have forgotten that part of the deck was closed. In order to load, passengers climb through a window and over a ramp made of deck chairs. Madeleine Astor, the 18-year-old pregnant wife of John Astor enters the boat. Her husband tells her 'You'll be all right. You are in good hands. I'll meet you in the morning.' She huddles in the boat wondering if she had now become a fiancée, wife, pregnant, and possibly a widow all within one year. Madeline is joined in #4 by her friends Marian Thayer and Eleanor Widener. Lowered with 40 people, #4 is the only lifeboat to immediately try to row back to the sinking site and pick up passengers. They are able to rescue six or seven. Some of those rescued survive and some do not.

Collapsible C is the first of the Engelhardt collapsibles to leave *Titanic*. She departs with 44 people after her sides are raised, the boat attached to the davits and lowered. Purser McElroy and Murdoch fight off a group of stewards and third-class passengers trying to board the boat. Bruce Ismay assists in finding women and children for the boat. After all women within sight are loaded, Ismay invited his friend William Carter and several other men to join him taking the empty seats. The jump in as it is lowered away. Carter has already put his family in another boat and is determined to take this opportunity. Several Chinese third-class passenger-seamen on the way to berths on a ship leaving out of New York are found in the boat as well. Launching at 2:00 a.m., the *Titanic* has only about twenty minutes to live. Ismay will live with his decision to enter Collapsible C for the rest of his life.

Collapsible D offers only 47 empty seats while there are still over 1,500 people left on the stricken liner at 2:05 a.m. Coming through a circle of crewmen protecting the boat are two small boys brought forward by a man using a false name. Kidnapping his children from his estranged wife, he is bringing them to America to start fresh. He has bundled up the boys – two and four years old – for warmth and kisses them goodbye. They find seats but are unable to communicate. Sitting terrified and alone, they speak only French. The boat is rapidly lowered with only 25 people.

Struggling to remove Collapsible B from the top of the officers' quarters, the boat has crashed through the makeshift ramps and landed upside down on the deck. *Titanic*, in her final five minutes of life, drops lower and lower allowing the ocean to wash the upside-down boat off the deck. Marconi operator Bride becomes trapped underneath the boat, breathing in jerky panicky gulps in the air pocket under the hull. Several dozen freezing swimmers attempt to climb on the overturned boat. Bride finds his way to the surface and succeeds in mounting the swaying boat and helps the boat's officer organize the rescued into two parallel rows on either side to balance the boat. Slowly during the dark night, the air pocket underneath diminishes bit by bit allowing the boat to sink lower and lower into the freezing water. Several succumb to the water as it rises and slide to the depths in death. Boats 4 and 12 take some of the freezing people into their boats. By some accounts, Jack Phillips, the indefatigable Marconi man who had stayed at his post far past the margin of his own personal safety, perishes from this boat while others say he never reached the boat at all.

Collapsible lifeboat A also washes from the deck as *Titanic* takes her final plunge. There was no time to completely raise her collapsed sides. It drifts partially underwater. Rhoda Abbott –

the only woman to survive after being thrown in the water – is washed from the *Titanic*'s deck holding her two boys' hands. Her mother's grip breaks loose in the swirling waters of the sinking, and both her sons are lost. She is pulled into Collapsible A to survive. As one by one occupants freeze and die in the semi-submerged boat, they are gently put over the side into the sea. By morning, about a dozen people still shiver feebly in the boat. Three of the dead are left in the boat to drift with the ocean swell well past the rescue of the living.

Just over seven hundred people will be alive to greet the dawn. 39% of the first-class passengers perish, 58% of second, and 76% of the third-class will not see the dawn. Of the crew, over 76% perish that night. All will be affected and some impoverished as all their worldly wealth sinks to the bottom. Young females on the honeymoon of a lifetime go from newlyweds to widows in one night. People like Anna De Messmacker know her last sane moments as she steps into lifeboat 13 without her husband. All remember the sounds of *Titanic*'s sinking. Explosions, yelled directions by the officers, but mostly the screams from the water and the sound of a collective groan from the lifeboats when so many husbands and sons slide into the depths. Only a handful of lifeboat occupants know that that *Carpathia* is aware of *Titanic*'s plight and is steaming to her aid. Lifeboat 14 knows that help is out there somewhere. Collapsible B knows from Marconi man Bride of a prospective savior on the way to them. Most of the survivors only know of the cold, the water slowly rising over their feet, and the silent blackness of the night, and their losses.

What is the fate of Captain Edward John Smith, a forty-year sea veteran, witnessed by passengers on the sinking ship? Depending on the eye-witness account given - and sworn to be accurate – he was on the bridge awaiting his fate as the ship's Captain in command and responsible for the thousands of passengers and crew now in peril of their lives. Or he was jumping off the ship at the last moment to commit suicide. Or swimming to a lifeboat with a rescued child. Once again swimming with a struggling woman in his arms, placing her in a lifeboat, and then vanishing into the dark as he swims away. He is seen being placed on a raft by two *Titanic* crewmen, but then jumping off and swimming out of sight. He is seen trying to soothe the passengers telling them there was no danger and to go back to their staterooms. He is said by many to have shot himself. He is said to have attempted to shoot himself twice but was interrupted. He tries a third time but is interrupted by Chief Officer Wilde. According to that witness, Wilde takes Smith's revolver away from him and shoots himself without any mention of the eventual fate of the Captain! He is 'known' to have shot two men and then shot the lookout in the crow's nest. He is most often said to be on or near the bridge before disappearing forever. He will never be seen again – alive or dead.

"Get up, the *Titanic* has hit an iceberg and is sinking. We are going rescue her passengers!"

The sound of pounding feet and scraping and banging above the Carpathia's passengers' heads after midnight wakes the light sleepers and worries many. Those closest to the top deck can plainly hear crew sweating and swearing at the lifeboat mechanisms above them as they shake the sleep from their eyes. Is the *Carpathia* sinking? Why are the boats being readied? Dressing quickly several passengers ask scurrying crewman and stewards what is amiss. Despite orders, some speak of rushing to help the *Titanic*, who is in distress. Dr. Blackmarr, one of the first to emerge on the cold upper deck sees it strewn with lifebelts, breeches buoys, and blankets. The sides of the *Carpathia* are lined with rope ladders. Two lifeboats are being made ready for lowering and their crews are assembling at their stations. It is very cold.

"Dr. Blackmarr, I am Dr. Arpad Lengyel. Captain Rostron told me you might be able to assist us. We are on our way to *Titanic*. I don't know her exact situation, but I know she has hit a berg and has asked for immediate assistance. We are now heading toward her as fast as this old girl can go. The other two doctors have first and second-class responsibilities. I have the third class, which has the most people and therefore I am hoping you might be able to assist."

"Indeed, I will Dr. Lengyel. Tell me what assistance you require from me."

"I have the surgery in steerage near the lowest entrance into the ship. I assume that is where anyone we pick up will enter the ship. Outside of my medical duties, I will also need to classify and assign any survivors where they will stay on this ship. I am preparing alleviatives, dressings, stretchers, splints, cognac and whiskey, pots of tea and coffee as well as food. Thankfully, our fever ward of 32 beds is empty so that will be where we take those who require the most care. I am assuming and hoping none of this will be necessary as I assume we will be ferrying passengers from *Titanic* to *Carpathia* who will be well and whole. However, Captain Rostron seems very concerned, and he is better informed than I."

"Let us hope this is the case. However, young Mr. Cottam the Marconi man has become something of a mentor to the young man who is traveling with us, and he informed me as he passed my cabin that it is quite serious."

Blackmarr and Lengyel finish all preparations including extra blankets and sterilizing instruments to be prepared for any eventuality. Going up on deck, they see the railing reflectors set up to light the surface of the water around the ship. All lookouts on the ship have been doubled. Canvas sacks, ropes, pulleys, and blocks are already set in position, and they can see Captain Rostron pacing from bridge wing to wing impatiently.

Father Albert Hogue is also watching the 'Electric Spark's energetic movements. While the sailors are dashing from deck to deck making preparations, the rest of the world seems calm and peaceful. A sky full of stars above and a gentle sea only moved by the wake of *Carpathia* shuddering along apace. A quick question thrown at a fast-moving crewman about the ship's speed receives a response thrown over his shoulder as he hurries past. "Not sure Padre. I heard up to 18 knots, which is faster than this old girl has ever run, God help us, and right into an ice field too!" Just past 3:00 a.m., the sky begins to show the first tinge of dawn. Calls come from lookouts about a brief green or blue light showing low on the horizon ahead. As the skies brighten a bit more, ice bergs of every size and shape appear all around. Rostron is dodging in and out of the wheelhouse as he steers the ship around the bergs. The crew can feel the excitement and speak of the 'old girl' feeling the excitement as well.

Just near 4:00 the first lifeboat is sighted and is greeted joyfully by *Carpathia*'s whistle. Less than half full, the first lifeboat slowly rows through the dawn chop on the sea towards her rescuer. In the breaking light of day, other distant lifeboats can be seen – some full – some more than half empty – some almost awash. The prepared ropes, bosun's chairs, and ash bags are soon busily employed hoisting the frozen occupants to *Carpathia*. Boat by boat starting at 4:10, the living remnants of the great liner *Titanic* embrace the solid decks of the 'friendly and comfortable' *Carpathia*. Her moment has arrived.

Four hours. Four hours of a kaleidoscope of images. White strained faces staring up the tall sides of *Carpathia* as lifeboats come alongside. Curious stares at the approaching boats from the *Carpathia* passengers lining the railings high above. *Titanic* lifeboat occupants struggling with freezing hands to row towards their rescuer. Captain Rostron constantly maneuvering his ship to close the distance to the bobbing boats. Ropes and slings placed around the shivering victims so they could be lifted to decks of the Cunarder. Small children being put inside bags and hoisted up, bringing some of the few cries from the found. Sounds of the small chop on the water lapping against *Carpathia* along with occasional cracking sounds from the surrounding icebergs. The rattle of oar locks as a boat approach. Victims refusing medical treatment to line the rails and look for husbands and sons who must be – they say over and over – in another boat. Muted whispering from the watchers above as lifeboats approach full, half-empty, and containing those already dead. A small child, pulled from a lifeboat, asks for a pencil and writes a note saying 'Daddy, we don't know what is keeping you. We are on this boat. We arrived before you and want you to come here.'

One of the last boats to approach, Lifeboat 14 slowly finds her way to safety. She is towing the struggling Collapsible D. Boat 14 has put in an eventful night with passenger transfers and rescues. It was secured to the towering side of *Carpathia* with the shivering Hadnots seated with other passengers – both the living and the dead. Nellie Hadnot needs assistance to be lifted. Elizabeth secures herself and follows her mother to safety. Blankets, warm drink, and the offer of a cabin are theirs within minutes of setting their feet on the deck. Safety and warmth are thankfully theirs, but the loss was crushing. Most of their belongings and money to get started in Ohio are over two miles down on the bottom of the Atlantic. Those things seem inconsequential now. The head of the enterprise, the one who had created and made the mission in India thrive, the doting father and loving husband, Reverend Allen Hadnot is gone. Neither Nellie nor Elizabeth has any realistic hopes of other rescue boats or that anyone could still be still alive out there somewhere. They heard the screams grow quiet after the sinking. No one could still live who weren't in the boats, and the boats are all accounted for. He is gone.

After the last lifeboat - #12 - is emptied about 8:15 a.m., the Leyland Lines *Californian* puts in her belated appearance. With the *Carpathia* currently not sending or taking wireless signals, hand flags exchange the information about *Titanic*'s sinking and the just-completed rescue of seven hundred survivors. Missing the first cry for help before shutting down for the night, *Californian* has only received news of the event from *Frankfurt* around dawn. Slowly tiptoeing through the ice, she arrives on the scene in time to be asked by Rostron to remain in the area and look for any bodies. Many explanations, accusations, and justifications will swirl around Captain Lord and the actions of his ship; that the *Titanic* veered to port after hitting the berg making her deck lights difficult to see from *Californian*. That the rockets lighting the night sky over *Titanic* were only company signals and not cries for help. That the action of *Titanic* sinking into the sea was actually seen as an unknown steamer sailing directly away from the *Californian*. Captain Lord – master of the *Californian* – in a decision he will carry with him forever decided he had enough information about the rockets. Without getting any response to the signal lamp, he decides not to rise from his nap on the chart room settee and investigate for himself or ask the wireless operator to investigate. Now the S.S. *Californian*, 6,223 tons and an average full speed of 12 knots, can only search for bodies. And she is even unsuccessful at that.

Closeted in Dr. McGhee's cabin, J. Bruce Ismay sits thinking about the might have beens after officially notifying White Star of what happened by wireless. Unexplainably, it would not be received for two days.

Deeply regret advise you Titanic sank this morning fifteenth after collision iceberg, resulting serious loss life further particulars later. Bruce Ismay

"Mr. Ismay, do you concur that we should remove ourselves directly back to New York, or some other port? I do not think we should take *Olympic*'s suggestion of transferring the *Titanic* passengers to her. I believe that would be more trauma for them to be put into lifeboats again for the transfer, and to an almost identical ship to the one they just evacuated. It would also require us to remain in this ice-filled area longer, which I have no desire to do. We certainly cannot continue to our scheduled Mediterranean destinations in the current situation. I also don't believe Halifax is a viable option, so New York does seem the best option. That was after all the destination of *Titanic*."

"I agree Captain Rostron. Do as you deem best."

"Very well. I plan to steam southwest to get out of this ice field and then on to New York. I think we should have a short Divine Service before leaving the site though. If you care to join us the service will be held in the first-class dining saloon."

"No Captain. I will remain here in my cabin."

"Very well sir."

Captain Rostron and Father Roger Brooke Taney Anderson, an Episcopal priest from Baltimore, hold two Divine services this sad day. As *Carpathia* steams gently and reverently around the so-called island of cork, deck chairs, and other miscellaneous remnants of the great ship, thanks are given for the lives of the rescued and absolution offered to those souls now departed. Later in the day at 4:00 pm, twelve hours after the first boats were spotted, Father Anderson holds a service to commit the bodies to the sea of those brought aboard from the boats dead or that had died shortly after being brought on board the *Carpathia*. A door in the side of the liner is opened and a gangway is let down. The bodies are lowered to this platform and covered with a British flag before being uncovered and carefully pushed off, making as little splash as possible. *Carpathia* brings in her lifeboats, which had been swung out ready to lower, home to their accustomed resting places. Six of the *Titanic*'s boats are brought up to the foredeck, and seven are carried slung overside in the davits. She has no room for the rest. They will be left to drift on the currents.

"Mr. Bisset, the *Californian* will remain on-site to search further, so we will leave her to her work. Bear away to the southwest. Take us out of the ice."

"Aye, sir. This may take hours though to clear this lot. I have never seen so much ice this far south."

"I agree. Let us make haste but with care. I am quite sure the people we picked up have seen quite enough ice for a lifetime. We will make our way at best possible speed to New York once we see our way clear of this."

Three hours later, the ship has finally cleared the ice and points her bow towards Pier 54, where she departed from four short days ago, Harold can already see the immense amount of work he will have on his equipment table in the upcoming days. He is waiting for the list of all surviving passengers so he can send it out. Some of the newly rescued are already making their way directly to his little house atop the 2nd class smoke room to inquire about sending a wireless message to their loved ones, attempting to bypass the purser for speed and economy. The world outside of *Carpathia* is wreathed in confusion and the messages of concern for *Titanic* are filling the air. Some Harold can read and require his response. Some are sent from stations out of range of his antiquated equipment and vanish without an answer.

White Star New York to Captain Smith Titanic

Anxiously waiting information and disposition passengers

White Star New York to Olympic

Endeavour communicate with Titanic and ascertain time and position. Reply as soon as possible.

MKC Olympic to New York

Since midnight when her position 41 N and 50.14 W have been unable to communicate with her. We are now 310 miles from her nine am under full power. Will inform you at once if hear anything

MKC Olympic to New York

Parisian reports Carpathia in attendance and picked up twenty boats of passengers and Baltic returning to give assistance

New York to Olympic

Thanks your message. We have nothing from Titanic but rumored here that she proceeding slowly Halifax but cannot confirm.

Carpathia to Olympic

We received distress call from Titanic at eleven twenty and proceeded right to spot. On arrival at daybreak we saw ice 25 miles long apparently solid Quantity of wreckage and number of boats full of lives. We raise about six hundred and seventy souls. Titanic has sunk. She went down in two hours Captain and all engineers. We have two or three officers aboard and the second Marconi operator. Fear absolutely no hope searching Titanic's position. Left Leyland SS Californian searching round. Not certain of having got through Please forward to White Star also to Cunard Liverpool and New York.

Am returning New York.

Olympic to Carpathia

Kindly inform me if there is the slightest hope in searching Titanic position at daybreak. Agree with you on not meeting. Will stand on present course until you have passed and will then haul more to southward. Have you communicated disaster to our people at New York or Liverpool or shall I do so and what particulars can you give me to send. Sincere thanks for what you have done. Haddock

Carpathia to Olympic

Fear absolutely no hope searching Titanic position. Left Leyland SS Californian searching round. All boats accounted *for and about 675 souls saved crew and passengers. Latter nearly all women and children. Titanic foundered about 2.20 am Not certain of having got through please forward to White Star also to Cunard Liverpool and New York and that I am returning New York. Rostron.*

After being awake all day and night, and now day again, Harold is pulled like a magnet towards iron to the smell of coffee and hot food. He has been awake for more than two days with no end in sight. Piling his plate high with food to help carry him through the vast pile of work awaiting him, he is filling a cup with steaming hot coffee when he feels a gentle tug on his uniform sleeve.

"Mr. Cottam? Is that you sir?"

His first over-tired instinct to snap back at the intrusion is muffled by the sound of the small polite voice. The mesmerizing ice-blue eyes are instantly recognizable. But she is no longer a child but starting to bloom into a very young woman. A very beautiful woman. Still oh so slight but showing just enough early womanhood to make a grown man catch his breath. Still, she is so terribly young, and he should not be having such thoughts about her. His thoughts and emotions war with each other as he tries to compose himself.

"Miss Hadnot. Is that truly you? What are you doing here? I mean, were you and your family on the *Titanic*? I had thought you were in India."

"Yes, it is I. We were indeed on the *Titanic*. We were going home to America."

"Are you alright? Were you hurt?"

"No, I am fine and unhurt."

"Is your mother all right as well?"

"She was not physically injured, sir."

"And your father? Is he with you?"

"No, he is no longer with us Mr. Cottam."

"Were you all traveling together on *Titanic*?"

"Yes. He is no longer with us."

Chapter Five

REFUGE AND REGRET

The quiet is deafening. Just the sad sounds of ropes rattling through pulleys and oars clumping and clattering down inside the lifeboats. An occasional grinding sound of a wood boat scraping against the steel hull. Quiet commands and responses are the only human sounds rising above the muted whispering sound from the passengers lining the rails of the *Carpathia*. The scenery is breathtaking. The soft dawn light is growing into a warm red glow. Icebergs everywhere in sight are taking on the hues of the sky in an ever-changing display of beautiful danger. Captain Rostron stands erect on the bridge wing supervising the rescue of lifeboat after lifeboat and adjusting his ship's position to keep it from harm. One large berg has a long red streak that looks like paint on its side. Rostron lifts his cap, murmurs a quick silent prayer, and says what all the watchers are thinking, 'so wonderful to look at and so dreadful to touch.' As Second Officer Charles Lightoller takes a final look around Lifeboat 12 and sets foot on *Carpathia*'s welcoming deck, a ghostly sobbing moan arises from those watching. There will be no more. The last lifeboat with living souls in it has been emptied and most of the surviving lifeboats now rest on *Carpathia*. While virtually all the first-class women aboard *Titanic* have found the safety of the Cunard ship, a total of almost 80% of all male passengers and crew – and almost half of the children - of the largest man-made moving object on the earth will never set foot on land again. Now with almost double her original complement on board, *Carpathia* steams slowly around the floating bergs searching in vain for something, someone, anyone. The friendly *Carpathia*, on her way to the sun and warmth of the Mediterranean and Adriatic, is now a cold and dark ship of widows and orphans.

Rostron's preparations have made his ship completely ready to receive her new charges. Warming drinks, blankets, and gentle voices help the newly arrived. Those needing medical attention – less than expected considering the circumstances – are moved to the hospital by medical staff and stewards. Some dazed passengers are escorted to cabins already voluntarily given up by *Carpathia* passengers or to other occupied cabins to fill the last of the empty beds. But many from the sunken ship resist any assistance in order to find an open spot at the rails of the ship to search for their loved ones. There must be more lifeboats or another ship. Nellie Hadnot is one of those who line the rail in vain hope. There must be more.

"Mother? Mother?"

"Mother, this is Mr. Cottam. Father and I met him years ago. He is the wireless man on this ship."

"Mother??"

"Mrs. Hadnot, I am pleased that you are safe. Please call me Harold."

The small woman huddling under several plaid blankets doesn't look away from the sea as she stands shivering at the rail oblivious to her daughter's voice.

"There must be other lifeboats. He might have been picked up by another ship."

"Mother, here is Mr. Cottam. He works on this ship, and he met Father years ago."

Turning, the same bright blue eyes as her daughter stand out sharply from her strained white face.

"You know my husband?"

"Yes, Ma'am. We met once years ago."

"You know my husband? Have you seen my husband?"

"Yes, Ma'am. I know your husband."

"Have you seen my husband? I have looked at every boat that came to this ship, but I have not seen him, but he must be on another part of this ship or on another ship. Have you seen him?"

Catching a signal from Elizabeth, Harold answers, "No Ma'am. However, I am required to stay near my workstation and so have not been over our whole ship this morning. Perhaps he is here somewhere. Elizabeth, why don't you get your mother settled and warm and then come back and we will check for your father. I will be in the Marconi house right up there between those boats. If I am busy, I will see to it that a steward helps you look for the Reverend."

"Yes, certainly a steward. There must be one nearby that can help me find my husband."

"Yes, Mother. We will look everywhere. Let us find a place that where we can get you warm and something to eat."

Stewards, doctors, crewmen, and passengers assist the newly added passengers to *Carpathia*. First-class passengers are being escorted to the first-class cabins or individual bunks in those cabins yielded up by existing passengers until they were full and then they will overflow to fill the more numerous second-class staterooms. *Titanic* carried many more first-class passengers than the *Carpathia* has first-class cabins. Rescued second-class passengers fill the remaining second-class cabins and the officers' cabins, while *Titanic* steerage passengers – who have suffered the highest losses by far – are filling every possible open spot in the third-class accommodations or the makeshift arrangements in the public rooms. Men with no cabins fill the smoke rooms while the women fill the dining saloons and library. *Carpathia*'s lady passengers are digging deep into trunks and suitcases for extra clothes and personal items for their new cabin mates. People had been dressed in everything; evening formal attire to nightgowns or hastily grabbed items of uncertain warmth and even gender. One male passenger arriving shivering in only a bathrobe is quickly fitted out from passengers' suitcases.

Elizabeth and a passing steward combine to pry Nellie away from the railing of the ship and to make her way to the second-class cabin the newly made two-person family will share with the current *Carpathia* occupants. The steward gently supports Nellie as they find their way through the unfamiliar ship. At every turn, she looks at him and asks, "Have you seen my husband?"

Everywhere through the ship, the stewards, stewardesses, and the medical staff circulate through the freshly rescued giving what aid they can. A warm drink – often laced with something stronger than coffee – is handed out. Blankets and clothing offered by others are gratefully accepted. Cuts and bruises are tended. The more seriously injured are taken to the ship's hospital. Those giving aid speak quietly and listen to the stories tumbling from the survivors. Few crewmen will speak at length hoping to sell their stories to the press and the *Titanic* officers will not talk at all. They have their jobs to consider. Passenger stories that will not be shared in a short time when the conventions of the polite society take over are now spilling out with raw emotion.

Only 24 years old, Pauline Aubart, had boarded *Titanic* with a trunk for her hats, one of dresses, and one entire trunk for lingerie, including 12 sets of knickers. She had said on leaving Paris that 'One does not come from Paris and buy her clothes in America. This is understood is it not?' Twenty-four of what she called night costumes of silk lace, corsets, and corset-covers along with a gold bag with sapphires, a purse with emeralds, and a tiara of 'brilliants'. She also boarded the brand-new White Star liner with her maid Emma and her lover. She was the mistress of Benjamin Guggenheim, the second richest man of the array of wealth on the ship. She had been a nightclub singer in Paris and she a married Jewish man retired from his vast mining and smelting holdings and partially retired from his marriage. Speaking no English, she pours out her loss in French to any who will listen. All her belongings, her lover, Guggenheim's valet, and chauffeur - her friends – are now all gone, as are her hopes for the future. Some of her fellow occupants of Lifeboat 9 had considered her frantic and overly emotional during the night, and now even though safe on the comforting decks of the *Carpathia*, she still teeters on the edge of a complete breakdown at the thought of the totality of her losses.

Even younger – only 22 years old – silent film star Dorothy Gibson and her mother are quickly approached and offered a cabin to share with *Carpathia* passengers James Lowell and his wife. One of only 28 in Lifeboat 7, Dorothy had been mumbling over and over for all to hear on *Titanic* and in the lifeboat 'I will never drive my little grey car again.' Given to her by her married lover film producer Jules Brulatour, the little grey car was all she spoke of except to join the others voicing their disagreement with any thought of returning to pick up those freezing to death in the water. Hoboken, New Jersey-born Dorothy had been a Broadway singer and dancer and was now a well-known silent film star. In between her ramblings about the little grey car, she makes her plans for the immediate future. A bit of breakfast, a long day and night's sleep, and then to find a way to let her lover know she is alright. After that, she quietly reasons with herself that maybe she can turn this tragedy to her advantage. After all, she almost died! Maybe a screenplay? Yes, she will start writing her epic saga after sending word of her survival and devotion to her married lover in New York.

Two members of Collapsible boat C are faring very differently on board the rescue ship. When pulled up from the boat fifteen minutes before 6:00 am J. Bruce Ismay and William Carter are two of the men who occupied the precious life-saving seats in the lifeboat. Stepping into their places of safety from the sinking *Titanic*, both had been working to fill the boat with women passengers before it was launched. Carter had taken his wife and children and left them waiting to load the yet-to-be-launched Lifeboat 4. He then left the group of men who had done the same like John Astor, George Widener, and John Thayer who were assisting their wives, to make his own plans. Ismay, after helping load several boats, stepped into Collapsible C and a lifetime of controversy. Now on *Carpathia*, both men have a large restorative breakfast and await developments - Ismay secreted in Dr. McGhee's cabin with a 'Do Not Knock' sign on the cabin door. With his dreams and huge company investment at the bottom of the sea, Ismay will not leave the cabin again during the voyage to New York. He will not eat solid food and will spend his days thinking of the past, of the future, of the screams of those who died in the water. Carter scans the sea from the deck of the ship for his family. After a warm breakfast, Carter sees lifeboat 4 approach the steep sides of the *Carpathia* with his wife and daughter looking hopefully upwards for rescue. Seeing them he shouts, "Where is my son?" The boy of 11 removes a large woman's hat which disguised his gender and yells back, "Here I am Father!" Carter's last view of his son when he left them at the lifeboat station was of young William Jr. handing John Astor the leash of his pet Airedale to hold with a promise to take care of him. His son's dog is lost, his valet is lost, and his chauffeur is lost, but he is saved. To his wife – in a statement that would come back at him - Carter simply says, "I had a jolly good breakfast. I never thought you would make it."

The decks, passageways, public rooms, and cabins of the *Carpathia* are a study in contrasts this morning in April.

Family reunions are held joyously and some of the rescued fall to their knees in prayer and thanksgiving as they set foot on the deck. Mr. and Mrs. Marshall, who had slept through the entire rescue, are awakened by a knock at their stateroom door. 'Mr. Marshall, your nieces wish to see you, sir.' Knowing his nieces are on the *Titanic* and that they had made Marconigram contact only a day earlier, Marshall is understandably confused by the appearance of his three bedraggled nieces at his door. Newly rescued Henry Harper – with his Pekinese pet - meets his old friend Louis Ogden and greets him simply by asking, 'How do you keep yourself looking so young?' Families separated in the chaos of the sinking and old friends and classmates meet again on the Cunarder in happy reunions. The Duff-Gordons arrange to have a picture taken of them and their boat crew on deck. All but the Duff-Gordons look away or stand unsmiling as the couple beams for the camera. Margaret Brown continues to care for other victims and along with the Countess of Rothes starts to organize relief efforts for those least able financially to recover from the sinking.

In pain, sorrow, and confusion, others nurse their physical pain and for many the knowledge that their loss was absolute. Of the twelve new brides on the Titanic, eleven now realize they are no longer newlyweds, but widows. Mrs. Churchill Candee, feminist and author, knows as she is being treated in the ship's hospital for the broken ankle she suffered when thrown into a lifeboat, that most of her friends that she had enjoyed so much were gone. She had watched Mrs. Straus wave goodbye to her as she stood on the deck with her husband after refusing to leave the ship without him. Her *Titanic* social group of Edward Kent, John Astor, and President Taft's military aid Archibald Butt are all gone. She assumes that her precious family heirlooms of a cameo of her mother and a silver flask with her family crest are lost too. She had given them to Mr. Kent, now also lost. Two boys, age four and two were on board came on board from Collapsible boat D.

They speak no English and have no parent or guardian. They are now considered orphans and will need care. Even when someone who speaks French is found, very little information is gotten from them except that their father had bundled them into warm clothes and put them together into the lifeboat after a tearful goodbye. Miss Margaret Hays of New York, who speaks French, cares tenderly for them the duration of the trip to New York.

Twenty-four hours ago, life had been very different from the people taking over the Captain's cabin on *Carpathia*. The sun was shining, as it was now, as people took the air on the promenade deck of the *Titanic*. Luncheon service was still underway as Eleanor and George Widener strolled the deck. They had stopped to chat with Bruce Ismay when the distinctive figure and white beard of Captain Smith came smiling up to them. No wonder he was called the Millionaire's Captain. As he chatted with the Wideners, he pulled a message form from his pocket and handed it to the managing director of White Star Lines. Bruce Ismay looked over the new ice warning from the *Baltic* and showed it to Eleanor and George. Making only a reassuring smile and shrug, he slid the form into his pocket as Captain Smith took over the conversation speaking of his anticipation for the upcoming special dinner in the À la carte restaurant in his honor. His favorite millionaires will be there; the Thayers, Archibald Butt, the Astors, the Wideners, and William and Lucile Carter will all be there. Elegant, intimate, and exclusive, the À la carte restaurant elevates the dining experience of first-class to a truly exceptional level. Exclusive menus, a vast staff to cater to every whim of the diners, and a string orchestra playing Puccini and Tchaikovsky make it an experience to remember. The dinner will be a shining event; impeccable service by liveried waiters serving the crème de la crème of society dressed in formal evening wear. Shortly after nine o'clock, when Captain Smith leaves to report to his bridge, the dinner breaks up with the ladies going to their staterooms and the men to the smoke room. What a glittering night! Hours later Madeline Astor, Marian Thayer, and Eleanor Widener all enter Lifeboat 4 as their husbands stepped back in obedience to the women and children only decree.

Now the three ladies, Madeline age 18, and pregnant, Marian 39 years old, and Eleanor as the oldest at 50 years old. All three – now widows. Rostron's comfortable quarters became a cabin of widows. Jack Thayer was found saved by his mother only on the *Carpathia* even though his lifeboat had been tied to hers during the night is already asleep in pajamas in a bunk supplied by a caring passenger. He had become separated from his family and jumped from the ship into the heaving frigid sea at the last moment and spent time on the hell called overturned Collapsible B before being transferred to a lifeboat. Marian is anxious to have her seventeen-year-old son Jack join her in the cabin when he finally wakes. John Astor had taken Madeline to the lifeboat station. However, the long wait for loading chilled her to the bone in her delicate condition so they spent some time warming themselves in the gymnasium as they waited. He even sliced open a spare lifebelt to show her how effectively it was made with all the flotation cork inside. He had moved to the open deck in one of his blue serge suits, gold cufflinks, and gold watch glittering. Lighting a cigarette, he had watched as his young bride was lowered to the sea. Widener, Astor, and Thayer had all stood silently together as they watched their wives disappear as the ropes played out through the pulleys. Now the conversation between Eleanor, Marian, and young Madeline starts and stops in the Captain's cabin. Only sobs end the unfinished thoughts and sentences.

Nearly unconscious when she is lifted to the warmth and safety of *Carpathia*, third-class passenger Rhoda Abbott is unable to walk after spending the night in the freezing water. She has no recollection of how long she was in the water before coming across the overturned Collapsible. She hung onto the sides of

Collapsible A with her last strength in water up to her hips. She had been washed from the deck of the *Titanic* with her sons Rossmore and Eugene. The young boys were unable to hang on and now her sons are gone. She has burns on her legs from some kind of explosion that she doesn't remember. Her clothing, a Salvation Army soldier's uniform, has to be cut from her. She is put to bed, unable to rise from her makeshift cot in the smoke room.

"Help!! Help!!"

"Rhoda, wake up! You are safe! This is Nellie. You are safe. Wake up. You are having the dream again."

Nellie had found Rhoda while searching all the public rooms for any word of her husband, and her missionary nature had called her to stay and befriend the sorely damaged Rhoda. She had sat next to her, combed some of the cork out of her hair, and quietly remained at her side until they were assigned to the same cabin. Now she sits next to her bed giving what comfort she can to the tortured woman.

"Each time I close my eyes, I see the same thing. I know that is it only a dream and not exactly what happened, but it is so terrible. I see it over and over. I am sitting in our cabin telling the boys about my life in England. Then suddenly the floorboards float up to my ears. Each time Gene is screaming more urgently for his life. I dive under towards the door only to find it bolted shut. The three of us are clinging to the ceiling searching for an escape route as the water closes in around us. I awake each time just as the water floods around my face."

"Mrs. Hadnot, I know that the boys and I jumped from the deck and were not locked in our cabin. I remember that much. I held onto their hands as tightly as I could, but they were pulled under. I didn't hear either Ross or Gene scream. They were just gone. There was nothing I could do. I swear it!"

"I understand Rhoda, and please call me Nellie. How old were your boys?"

"Rossmore was sixteen and Eugene younger. He just had his sixteenth birthday on March 31."

"And your husband?"

"We are separated. He is a retired boxing champion in England."

"Well, we may both have lost all the men that matter to us in this world Rhoda. I am still searching and praying for my husband, but no one has seen him or heard anything about him. I have not given up yet, but I……."

"I'm sorry Mrs. Had…. Nellie."

"I will stay near you, and we can pray and speak of our men together. Is that acceptable to you? My daughter was saved with me, and I will send word to her where I am. She will understand. She is, after all, a missionary's daughter."

MPA to Cunard

Am proceeding New York unless otherwise ordered, with about 800, after having consulted with Mr. Ismay and considering the circumstances. With so much ice about, consider New York best.

MPA to Associated Press

Titanic struck iceberg sunk Monday 3 am 41.46 N 50.14 W Carpathia picked up many passengers am proceeding New York. Large number icebergs and 20 miles field ice with bergs amongst. Rostron.

> **White Star New York to Commander Carpathia**
>
> What is your present position When do you expect reach New York? Anxiously awaiting names remaining additional survivors and crew
>
> Vitally important that we receive names balance survivors including third class and crew. Please do you utmost give us this information at earliest possible moment

The work has already piled up when Harold settles back into his chair in the Marconi shack. No one knows the limitations of his weak old-style Marconi system better than he does. He can't reach Cape Race which is only 350 miles from the *Titanic* death site. He certainly is unable to reach New York or any other land station. His best ally will be the approaching RMS *Olympic*. She has the most powerful transmitter in the region and is steaming east towards the disaster site at full speed. They will be in communication range by early afternoon and will cross paths by late afternoon. Harold has already sent a few messages to her before lunch. He answers a call for information from her as soon as he sits down and dons his earphones.

> Will send survivor names immediately we can. You can understand we are working under considerable difficulty. Everything possible being done for comfort of survivors. Please maintain stand by.

Within minutes, Harold begins conveying the ghastly news to *Olympic* for her information and to forward it to shore stations.

Titanic Captain, chief, first and sixth officers and all engineers gone. Also, doctor, all pursers, one Marconi operator and chief steward gone. We have second, third, fourth, and fifth officers and one Marconi operator on board.

For the next two hours, Harold fights off the effects of no sleep for 36 hours and sends the names of 322 first and second-class passenger survivors on board the *Carpathia*. The third class and crew survivors' lists will be sent when they are compiled and available, and when *Carpathia* is in contact with another powerful transmitter like the surviving sister ship of the sunken *Titanic*. *Olympic* sends out the horrific numbers and the world learns both the scale of the disaster and *Carpathia*'s name for the first time. She has plied the seas for years on her cargo/passenger routes in complete anonymity. In the space of a few hours that has all changed for her.

"I can't do everything at once. Patience please!!"

"I'm sorry. I did not mean to upset or disturb you."

The small silhouette of Elizabeth Hadnot fills the door to Harold's workplace. He had not heard her approach over the noisy clicking and electrical snaps of the equipment, and her quiet voice has startled him.

"No, please excuse me. I didn't mean to snap at you. Please come in. Maybe you can offer me a bit of sanity here."

"I doubt that. I don't have much of that for myself, much less some to share."

"I am very sorry Miss Hadnot. I have offended again. Please accept my apology. I am not usually so careless with my words. I plead tiredness. How is your mother doing? Has there been any word of your father?"

"Mother seems, well she seems – a bit better. She has found another survivor to care for which will help, I think. As to Father, no official word has been put out, but he is not anywhere on this ship that I can find. I told Mother I would check with you, but I have already checked. I knew you would be too busy with your duties to go dashing around this ship."

"Thank you. I will help in any way I can. Please come in."

"I don't want to disturb your work."

"No, you will not disturb me. In fact, I would appreciate your company. Perhaps you will keep me awake enough to be somewhat accurate in my messages. I have just finished sending the lists of people on this ship and am now waiting for instructions from my Captain as to how to proceed further."

"Thank you, Mr. Cottam. Then I will stay for a little while. I like this small house. It keeps me away from everything that is happening on the ship."

"Please Miss Hadnot, call me Harold. We don't seem to be that different in age compared to our first meeting."

Elizabeth – blushing furiously – gives him a nod and asks Harold to address her by her first name as well. "Would you mind terribly telling me how this all happened to *Titanic*?"

"I can only tell you what I know from my wireless. I do not know what caused the accident nor do I know anything about the actual sinking or the lifeboats."

"That is alright Mr…. Harold. I will never forget those parts. Ever."

"I am sorry Elizabeth. Are you sure you want me to go over all this with you?"

"Indeed. It will help me, I think. Besides, anything I can hear to blot out some of the sounds I remember from the sinking will be a gift."

"Very well then."

"It was only a streak of luck that I got the message at all. I had been up until 2:30, and the night before that until 3 o'clock. I had finished my day and was ready to turn in but decided to make one more try at Jack Phillips. He is the head Marconi man on *Titanic* and a friend of mine. I wanted to tell him he had messages waiting for him from Cape Cod. As soon as I messaged him though, he replied that they had struck a berg and to come at once. So, I got that message to my Captain, and we burned coal like a madman to get there. Our usual speed is 13 or 14 knots, but one engineer told me we had somehow been making between 17 and 18 knots. This old girl was really shimmying and shaking. Excuse me! It was a busy and confusing time. My set is an old-style with a limited range so the signals can come and go. I could hear Jack trying to work any ship within range. Sorry, working a ship means sending and receiving messages from that operator. Some would answer and some probably didn't hear the signals so didn't answer. Finally, he sent me that we should come quickly because the engine room is filling up to the boilers and they were putting the people in boats."

"I remember that part."

"That was the last message I got from him. I kept calling him and telling him we were on our way and to watch for our rockets. But I don't know that he ever got the later messages."

"Harold, were there other ships out there that could have helped us?"

"Well, Elizabeth there were other ships out there. I will tell you the other ships I was in contact with at different times, but I can only judge their distance by the strength of their signal. Plus, they have to have their systems energized with someone listening or they don't even know they are being called on for assistance. The *Californian, Parisian, Mount Temple, Birma, Frankfurt, Baltic, Virginian*, and even the distant *Olympic* all were within wireless range at one time or another during the night."

"Why didn't others come then?"

"I cannot be sure of all of them, but here are two examples; the *Californian* was shut down for the night and not receiving, and the *Olympic* – with her big powerful transmitter – was sending and receiving but hundreds of miles away. Much too far away to help."

"I see."

"What will you and your mother do now?"

"I will have to talk to Mother when she is able, but I must assume our plans are unchanged. Due to a death in the family, we are on our way to Henry County Ohio to take over my uncle's farm. Father and Mother were heartbroken about leaving the mission orphanage and all the children, but the family needed us. Also, Father was talking a bit more lately about us having been in India long enough and now that the mission was an operating church and orphanage, we should think about leaving it to the local people to run themselves. We will have to throw ourselves at the mercy of our relatives and their church though as everything we owned in this world was in our cabin on *Titanic*. Even this dress is borrowed."

"You look lovely in it nonetheless."

"Thank you, kind sir."

For such a direct young woman, Elizabeth blushes at the slightest discomfort and the pallor of stress in her face is now colored with a bright red blush. Harold matches that blush and is discovering a different side of himself in his attraction to this young woman. She has an uncomfortable hold on him. Since leaving his home in Southwell, his world has been Marconi and the camaraderie of his fellow Marconi men. Studies of electricity and magnetism, the apparatus of Marconi and diagrams of electrical connections, how to trace and repair problems, and the rules of the Radiotelegraph Convention had taken up the hours of his days. Not to mention having to have learned the regulations and behaviors of shipboard life. He was signed on to the ship's articles as a member of the crew and subject to the discipline of the Captain but worked for Marconi. Sometimes that balancing act took all his concentration as well. He had found no time for the tenderness, vulnerability, and strength of a woman. Until now.

The Marconi apparatus chatters to life startling them both.

White Star New York to Carpathia

It is of vital importance that we should have the names of the survivors of the Titanic that are onboard your steamer. Kindly wire to us in New York promptly.

"How many times do I need to send it out? What is wrong with those people?"

"You did say that this system has a somewhat limited range. Maybe they didn't receive it. How far can you transmit?"

"Well Elizabeth, for simple vertical sending and receiving antennas, the maximum working telegraphic distance varies as the square of the height of the antenna. And it varies with the power in watts of the unit as well. Understand?"

For the first time in many hours a smile, at the obvious attempt to impress her, creases the face of young Miss Hadnot as she simply looks at Harold and shakes her head.

"Not very far honestly. At least compared to the newer sets in ships like *Titanic* and *Olympic*. This is not a new or famous ship after all."

A steward gives a surprised glance at Harold's unusual companion in his normally private domain as he delivers a message form to be sent and leaves. The system once more explodes into sound and fury as an incoming message arrives.

"I will take this one message and then send one out, and then we can talk a bit more."

> *To Carpathia from White Star New York*
>
> *Cable ship Mackay-Bennett chartered by White Star scheduled to leave Halifax Noon 17 April to retrieve bodies Titanic last known position.*
>
> *Please confirm last known position*

> *To White Star New York from Ismay*
>
> *Most desirable Titanic crew about Carpathia be returned home earliest moment possible. Suggest you hold Cedric sailing her daylight Friday unless you see any reason contrary. Propose returning in her myself. Please send outfit of clothes including shoes for me to Cedric. Have nothing of my own. Please reply.*

Harold says nothing of the content of either of the messages to Elizabeth. Already people are moving on to recover bodies and craft their public responses and explanations of their actions before, during, and after the disaster. Harold's silence on the messages speaks loudly.

"Do you really think my father is lost? That there is no hope at all?"

"I'm sorry Elizabeth, but I honestly don't think there is much hope. I was in touch with any possible ship that had even a remote chance to assist in the rescue. I know where they all were and what their actions were. *Carpathia* was the only ship involved in rescuing any of the passengers. I am so terribly sorry."

"I know it is the truth. I have known it ever since the people in the water went quiet while we were in the lifeboat. But I trust you and needed to hear it said out loud."

"Ah, Mr. Cottam. I see you have a helper with you."

"Aye Captain. This is Miss Elizabeth Hadnot. I met her family years ago while I was on shore leave from the *Medic*. She and her father and mother were on the *Titanic*. She and her mother are now aboard with us."

"My sincere prayers for your family Miss Hadnot. I am very sorry for your loss. Mr. Cottam, I have strict instructions for you as we steam towards New York. First, every message from here on will be approved by me and sent under my authority. No messages are to be sent not authorized by me. Understood?"

"Aye, sir."

"Second, sending official messages regarding names of survivors aboard *Carpathia* and messages from those people to their loved ones will be your only priorities. Nothing else is important or will be processed by you. Understood?"

"Aye, sir."

"You will have every living person on this ship wanting to send out a message shortly. You will also have every newspaper and opportunist in the world trying to get information from you. We have already notified the Associated Press, Cunard, and White Star, so the rest can wait until we get to New York. I am sure you will have no time for them anyway, but I wanted to be very clear that the survivors' ability to contact their families is second only to official traffic across the wireless. If anyone gives you a fight on this, send them to me. Now I think it best this young lady goes to her cabin to rest. It has been a long and trying day for her. And you need to get ready for the deluge of people trying to get you to do their bidding. No matter what they say, remember my instructions."

"Aye, sir."

"Incidentally, young man, well done last night. If you had gone to bed as planned, or not handled the incoming traffic as you did, the losses would be much higher, including this pretty young woman. You have done credit to yourself and your profession."

"Thank you, sir."

"Goodnight to you both."

"Night Captain."

"Harold, if it is acceptable to you, I will look in on you tomorrow if you are not too busy. I must go back to check on Mother now and then attempt to get some sleep myself. Hopefully, I am tired enough to just sleep and not dream tonight."

"Goodnight Elizabeth. I am so awfully happy that you are well and safe. And here. I very much look forward to seeing you tomorrow."

A slight scent of carnations leaves the room with Elizabeth, even above the electric smell of the sparking equipment. How this is possible he has no idea. She certainly wouldn't have taken the time or thought to bring perfume along while trying to save her life. Putting that mystery away, Harold turns to his work and sits at his equipment table tapping away as *Carpathia* steams westward. It is a sleepless night for Harold – and many others on board the ship soon to be called the *Titanic* rescue ship

Heavy fog is followed by the crash of thunder and bright bolts of lighting as *Carpathia* steams through the heavy weather. Already traumatized survivors are jolted from their beds by the booming foghorn sounding and the explosive cracks of thunder. Many are convinced that the ship is in danger – more ice, more exploding rockets arching above the ship. Many of the silent and shaken huddle in their beds waiting for what the call to lifeboats once again. Eventually, the comforting rhythm *Carpathia* produced at her normal cruising speed soothes the survivors back to sleep.

She is once more the comfortable and friendly ship that is her true nature. Her unexpected meeting with destiny, her risky dash at breakneck speed through a threatening ice field, and the technical execution of the rescue of people from lifeboats in an ice-flecked sea are now all in her past. Her duty now is to heal and comfort the survivors and deliver them to their families. The crashing thunderstorm abates and the complete silence of nighttime on a ship at sea covers the decks and cabins of the Royal Mail Ship *Carpathia*.

The outside world is in a frenzy seeking information. Who lived – who died? Who amongst the elite of the world have found a watery grave? But on the *Carpathia*, it is a sea of quiet. Unable to send or receive at great distances, she cannot respond to everyone clamoring for information even if she wished. Captain Rostron has given his strict orders, but the public officials, the press, and friends of *Titanic* passengers do not know of his orders. They only know the frustrating silence coming from mid-ocean. Some on *Carpathia* are using the nighttime to organize funds to assist the less fortunate of the survivors. Thousands will be raised. Some are using the nighttime to propose a tangible means of rewarding the officers and crew of *Carpathia* for saving their lives. Thousands will be raised, and medals proposed. Some use the dark hours to compile a positive version of their behavior. Some are simply using these projects to avoid sleeping and dreaming. Rostron uses the time to plan his orders for their arrival at New York City; how to handle the press, how to replenish his ship, and how to continue his interrupted voyage to Gibraltar and beyond. Harold uses the nighttime to try to finish what work he can – reach what ships he can – before collapsing into a deep sleep fully dressed at his key.

RMS CARPATHIA

1903-1918

Hull # 274 under construction at Swan Hunter & Wigham

Newcastle upon Tyne, England

Second Cabin Entrance

SECOND CABIN DINING ROOM, T.S.S. "CARPATHIA."

Dining Saloon and Library

Carpathia lowering *Titanic* lifeboats in New York April 1912

Carpathia alongside Pier 54 in New York City April 1912

Arthur Rostron

Captain of the *Carpathia* during the *Titanic* Rescue

RMS *Carpathia*

William Prothero

Last Captain of the *Carpathia*

Carpathia sinking taken from the deck of U-55

Chapter Six

FINAL DESTINATION

"I hear you are acting queer."

Harold raises his head looking with bleary eyes at the familiar face smiling wanly at him.

"Well, Harold Bride! You are a sight! Good to see you old man. It has been a long time. I am very glad to see you safe."

"Cottam, you look almost worse than I."

"I don't think so, Harold. I am just tired from no sleep. But you - you are all bandaged up. Are you going to be alright old man?"

"Yes, so they tell me. I was actually quite lucky. I will tell you the whole story, but in short, someone was on top of me in the lifeboat and my feet were wrenched this way and that – all the while lying in the freezing water. Still, once again, I am quite lucky and they tell me I will be fine, eventually. After they pried my boots off when I got here, your Doctor McGhee checked me over and then bandaged me up. Time, he said, is what is needed for me."

"Well, I am quite glad to see you old man. I am glad you are safe. How about Phillips? Did he get off all right as well?"

"No, Jack is gone. I am still a bit wooly about exactly what happened to him, but I know he is not here on the *Carpathia*. The last I saw him for certain; he was heading aft from the Marconi room on *Titanic*. Some said he was on the Collapsible boat with me, but I am just not sure. I was fairly well out of things by that time."

"Very sorry to hear that news. I am glad you are safe though and I thank you for the visit."

"This is no visit, old man. Your Captain Rostron was told that you were acting queer from no sleep. He knew you needed help, and I knew I needed to stay busy, so here I am old man. Put me to use! The Captain also asked me repeatedly about some of the musicians he knew from past service on here that were on *Titanic*, but I couldn't tell him much except they played until the very end. I have not seen any of them on *Carpathia* and I think they are all gone. I suppose we will get everything sorted out and know for sure who lived and died by the time we reach New York."

"Well Marconi officer Bride, I can certainly use your help. We have a hellish job ahead of us. I will apologize in advance for my system. After that big powerful set you were used to, my old set here will tax your patience. Adding to that is everyone on this ship wanting to send a message, every shore station and passing ship breaking in to ask for information, and every family member of every person that was on *Titanic* is trying to call us directly for news. And I won't even talk about the newspapers.

Here is what is in store for us. At last count, I think I already have about 400-500 messages as yet unsent. At least the Captain has given strict orders that only service messages and messages from the survivors on board are to have priority. That will lighten the load a bit, but I am sure everyone else will be screaming at us for not answering them. Still, nothing will be lost if you take a few minutes and tell me about your experience. Those other people can wait. Tell me what happened to you. And to Phillips. Now give me those crutches and rest yourself. Put those feet up and tell me."

"Well, believe it or not, I slept right through the actual collision. I have heard it was pretty gentle unless you were forward or down below decks near the actual hit. I woke on my own and when I went into the workroom, Jack mentioned that he thought something was wrong with the ship. We had stopped for some reason. I took over the set to allow Jack to get a break. He had been going pretty hard with all the commercial traffic we had to Cape Race. Just a few minutes later Captain Smith came into our space and told us to get ready to send a call for assistance, but not to send it until he ordered us to. I remember Jack and I looked at each other as we realized that this might be serious. Needless to say, that was the end of any rest for Jack or me. Just a bit later the Captain was back and told us to send both the standard CQD and the newer SOS. I remember I made some effort at a joke-telling Jack to send the new SOS as it might be our last chance to use it. It was funny for a moment at least."

"I must have missed your first message when I was delivering my daily summary to the bridge."

"Yes, we didn't get the *Carpathia* at first as I remember."

"So, after one of my trips up to the bridge to deliver messages, I could see we were putting people off in boats. That is when we really realized how serious it was. I started scribbling a second copy of our procès-verbal, so Jack and I could each take one copy of our summary of messages with us when we left the ship. I don't know what happened to those two copies though. It all happened so fast at the end that they just disappeared. I am not sure if we even took them with us out of the Marconi room. Jack was still bashing away at the key even as the signal grew weaker and weaker. The Captain came back again and told us that the engine room was taking water and that we might not have power much longer."

"I remember. I got that message Bride. You know, I don't know if this will cause me trouble or not, but I got so busy working with you on *Titanic* and other ships that I completely gave up even trying to keep my log. I have no real record of all the messages coming in and going out. So, no procès-verbal log for either of us."

"Well, I tell you, Mr. Cottam. You should have seen Jack Phillips at work. Pounding away at his key, trying to adjust the spark, with all bloody hell breaking out all around us. He was so brave that I learned to love him that night as he sat calmly doing his work while everybody else was raging about. I will never forget the work of Phillips during those last awful fifteen minutes. As I looked out, the deck was awash, but Phillips kept on sending and sending, even after the Captain released us. I can't remember the Captain's exact words, but he told us we had done our duty and now it was time to fend for ourselves. Jack didn't listen but kept trying to send while I gathered our things to be on our way. He even kept sending when a stoker came in and tried to take his lifebelt right off him as he sat at the key! Well, I knocked that sod off of Phillips and he bashed him on the head, and we left him lying on the floor when we left."

"You say a black gang member tried to take his lifebelt right off his body?"

"Exactly. I had been trying to dress Jack in warm clothes and a lifebelt as he sent out the signals and had gotten him maneuvered into a lifebelt somehow. This sod was trying to strip it right off him as he sat! He didn't move after we knocked him about, so I don't know if we killed him or not; not that it really matters – the sod. We left him lying there. We both climbed up the roof of the officer's quarters and tried to get the Collapsible off. I am not sure what happened to Jack then and the next thing I knew I was trapped under the overturned boat in the water. I tell you, old man, finding yourself in freezing water with your head hitting the seats of an overturned boat above you brings you close to your maker. Somehow, I got out from under and a passenger – I think his name is Jack Thayer – helped me on the boat. He is just a young lad. I will have to find him and thank him. We sat holding each other's lifebelts to make sure neither of us slid off. I kept telling those on the overturned boat to hang on; that my friend Harold Cottam and the *Carpathia* were on the way. Don't give up. Eventually, those of us left alive on the Collapsible were transferred to other boats before we got to your ship. I tell you, my friend; your rockets soaring into the sky were very welcome sights to us in the boats."

"Good God man, what a story. I am so glad you survived. A lot of people have you and Jack to thank for their lives."

"Thank you, Harold. That is kind. But so many are lost. So many from that beautiful ship. And Jack especially. What a job he did. I will never forget."

"You shouldn't. We Marconi men met the imperative of the hour. At least most of us did."

"What do you mean?"

"Well, Cyril Evans was out here nearby as well. You remember Cyril, don't you?"

"I remember him. Cyril is out here somewhere now too? What ship is he on now?"

"Cyril is the sole operator on the *Californian*."

"He is? We only had brief contact with them, and Jack told them to stop interfering. They were blowing our ears off. I didn't recognize it was Cyril. Where was the *Californian*?"

"They were closer to you than we were, but he had shut down for the night."

"And they didn't see the *Titanic* all ablaze with lights? Sending up distress rockets? Signaling with the signal lamp? That was them? That was Cyril?"

"Yes. I don't know the details except that he was shut down before the crash. I don't know anything about what happened with seeing any rockets or anything – just the wireless. I almost was shut down as well. It was a close thing, Harold. A very close thing."

"Good God."

"Cottam, why don't you take a break and let me take the key for a bit. Go stretch your legs and bring us both some hot – really hot – coffee and we can work this together."

"Why thank you, Mr. Bride. I will do just that and return quickly."

Climbing down to the boat deck, Harold pauses at the deck rail and gives a large yawning stretch. Some of the *Titanic* survivors are spread around the decks of the ship. Bundled up and still trying to get warm, most are sitting silently. Some are exchanging their stories of survival and loss. He recognizes two small bundles of blankets approaching him.

"Mrs. Hadnot, Elizabeth, it is good to see you up and about this morning. I hope you are doing as well as can be expected."

"Have we met?"

"Mother, this is Mr. Harold Cottam, the Marconi man. You met him briefly just after coming on board. He is the man I told you about."

"Oh yes. I had forgotten. Please forgive me, Mr. Cottam. I have not had much sleep. I do not sleep well without my husband near me, and now with the dreams, it may be even more difficult. Have you by any chance received any news of other ships that may have picked up other passengers?"

"No Ma'am. I have not."

"Well God's will be done. I miss the Reverend terribly."

"Is there anything I can do for you? May I bring you something warm to drink?"

"Yes, young man. That would be nice."

"Miss Hadnot, if you would accompany me, I could use your help. I need to bring hot coffee to my new assistant and myself. I fear I don't have enough hands to accomplish that without your help."

"Gladly Mr. Cottam. We will return soon Mother."

Resting her arm through his revives and warms Harold completely. As they thread their way through groups of the rescued, he asks, "How is she doing?"

"A bit better. However, when she does doze, she wakes repeatedly asking if I can hear the screams. Then she drops off and awakens again asking if I can hear the band playing. I have a hard enough time myself trying to forget the sounds I heard from the lifeboat, without the questions being shouted out again and again. I hope she will be more at ease by the time we get to Ohio. I miss my Father already and don't want to lose my Mother as well."

"What are your plans in Ohio?"

"We have close family in a very small farming community in northwestern Ohio named Napoleon. It is supposed to be a nice town near a canal and railroads which help it prosper. Father said it was a growing community with many small children and families. There are Lutheran churches in the area, both English, and German-speaking, so we should be welcomed and have a good church life. We will be living on a farm. I have never lived on a farm or in America for that matter. It will be very different from my life up to now. But I guess after this trip my whole life will be different forever no matter what the farm is like. Father was always there for me. Any time I needed anything, from that time years ago when I almost drowned to this past Sunday night, he was there. I will miss him so awfully. The thought of growing older without him to talk to is unbearable."

Considerably surprising himself, Harold slowly turns and embraces Elizabeth tightly in full sight of other passengers. She presses herself against him and sags deep in his arms for a moment before drawing away. She smiles a very adult smile at him when she sees the blush filling his face under his uniform cap. He can feel every contour of her in his memory on their walk back to the Marconi house with hands filled with steaming coffee cups.

"Mr. Bride, this is Miss Hadnot. She is also from the *Titanic*. She consented to help me carry hot coffee to you."

"Pleased to meet you, Miss. I don't recall meeting you before, but we are usually chained to our desk tapping away during a voyage and don't meet many passengers."

"Pleased to meet you, Mr. Bride. I do hope you heal quickly and feel better soon. Harold, I must return to my Mother. She will wonder what has become of me and her coffee."

"You must be careful Miss Hadnot if you call for Harold. You see, my first name is Harold as well. We will confound everyone on this ship with two Marconi men named Harold at the same time."

"Very true Mr. Bride. I will be very careful of what I say to whom. It was nice to meet you and I am sure I will see you again. I hope your feet feel better very soon. Goodbye for now. And to you Mr. Cottam, thank you for your caring and concern on our walk. It was much needed. I will go back to Mother now but will see you again as soon as possible." Her tell-tale carnation scent lingers for a moment in the room after she leaves.

"Mr. Cottam, she is young, but you have a real woman on your hands there in Miss Hadnot. She is obviously in love with you. You must be quite the charmer to have her smitten in the course of one walk."

"Nonsense. Nobody is smitten. Besides, I met her and her father years ago, so it was not just one walk. Now let us get back to work. Want me to take the key now?"

"You know Harold, I got engaged myself just a couple of weeks before we started sea trials."

"Congratulations!"

"I hope so. I like Mabel well enough, but she pretty much nagged me into the engagement before we went to sea. I suspect she wants to have someone to brag over more than she wants me. I am having second thoughts about it."

"Well, I do wish you happiness, whatever that entails. As for me, I shouldn't think of Miss Hadnot as a lifetime partner. She is barely into her teen years. But I cannot stop thinking about her either. She is an old soul for her age and very attractive."

"You know that often on board ship or in a stressful situation, relationships can progress at an artificially speedy pace. Maybe you will forget her, and she forget you after we reach New York."

"Maybe, but I doubt it. I have already tried that. Say, Harold, this sounds awkward between us with both having the same first name. I can guarantee that the crew and passengers will be confused between us. Do you have any kind of nickname?"

"Yes, but it is mostly used by my Mother and some of the females in the family. She calls me Harry."

"Do you have objections to myself and others using that for the duration of the trip to New York?"

"None."

"Well Harry, I met Elizabeth years ago by chance while shipping on the *Medic*. She was much younger then, but even back then she already seemed an old soul; and very much too interesting to me for her age. That hasn't diminished, but only grown stronger now that she is older."

"You have it bad, old man, don't you?"

"Harry, can we speak of something else? Or just get to work on this stack of message forms?"

"Alright old man, alright. But before we start sending again, one thing has been bothering me. I hate to even speak of it, and don't worry, it doesn't involve your love life. I know there are just over 700 souls on board from *Titanic*. I know I was almost out of my head when I was pulled aboard, but where are the rest of the people? I haven't heard of bodies being taken aboard except just a few from one of the boats and some of the others I have spoken to from *Titanic* also say there were no bodies on to be seen in the sea."

"My Captain says he only saw one body in the water. I have no idea about the rest. The reasons I have heard whispered about are vastly different. Some say the bodies all sank with the ship and will only rise to the surface later which puzzles me. Some say they were there but not seen because their white lifebelts look like ice or the chop of the sea surface. Others think that currents carried them away from us and some wonder if we weren't actually in the same position as the sinking considering the drift of the current and wind when we picked up the boats. Or possibly the positions figured after the collision on the *Titanic* weren't dead on. The *Californian* didn't report any bodies to us either before she left the area, so I really don't know."

"That is a mystery. I saw Fourth Officer Boxhall and he said the same thing as your Captain. Just one body seen. Still, I wonder what happened to all those people. I know they weren't all inside the ship when she went down. I heard the sounds and saw the sights in the water."

"Harry, I think there are some things about this disaster that people will still be debating long after we are dead and gone. A hundred years from now, people will swear that they saw this or saw that – heard this or heard that – or know for certain that this happened or that happened. We certainly can't solve the mysteries now. Maybe we should put it aside for now and get back to these messages. You get yourself propped comfortably on my bed, rest your feet, and I will take the key and start to worry this pile of paper down."

"Agreed Mr. Cottam. Let's get back to work."

Have reports you and sisters safe. Is father with you? Hurry answer

Congratulations on escape. Exceedingly anxious know whether Isidor Straus and wife are saved

Glorious rejoicing. Belief always made us know you are safe. Love

Are you and Sam safe and well?

Is Benjamin Guggenheim aboard? Please answer without delay

Parents anxiously waiting news. Answer to me

Have you any news of my Father Col John Astor

Sir Cosmo and lady Duff Gordon safe

Every boat watched for Father Mother. Not on Carpathia. Hope still

Don't be alarmed. Sydney may be on another boat

Father not seen. No hope. Arrive Carpathia New York

Hundreds of messages are being sent to and from the small Marconi shack grafted onto the boat deck of *Carpathia*. The two Harolds take turns at the key – taking most meals surrounded by the clattering of the wireless sparks. When one operator can no longer continue, he takes to the small bed and the other takes over the key. Mixed with the personal messages, White Star, Cunard, and even Marconi himself are trying to get information from the Cunarder.

White Star New York to Carpathia

Concise Marconigram account of actual accident greatly needed for enlightenment public and ourselves. This is most important

G Marconi to Carpathia

Wire news dispatches immediately to Siasconset or to navy boats. If this impossible ask Captain give reason why no news allowed to be transmitted. Is Colonel Astor aboard? Give me answer Head Office quick. Give this precedence

The tortured story of J. Bruce Ismay continues. By accounts from crew and passengers on *Carpathia*, Ismay never leaves his cabin. He is reportedly under opiates and sitting staring at the floor and unresponsive to others. Yet, a flurry of messages under his name stream towards New York regarding his impending arrival, and hopefully quick departure. He has a desperate desire to return the *Titanic* crew and himself to England as soon as possible. They were all signed with his so-called code name YAMSI to disguise his name from the listening world.

Carpathia to White Star New York

Send responsible ship officer and fourteen white star sailors on two tug boats to take Titanic boats at quarantine. Widener not aboard. Please cable wife am returning Cedric. YAMSI

Carpathia to White Star New York

Very important you should hold Cedric daylight Friday for Titanic crew. Think most unwise keep Titanic crew until Saturday. Strongly urge detain Cedric sailing her midnight if desirable. YAMSI

Carpathia to White Star New York

Most undesirable to have crew NY so long. YAMSI

Outside of the frenetic world of the Marconi house disoriented *Titanic* passengers relax on deck and adjust to their new reality. Some mix with *Carpathia* passengers and some keep to themselves; not yet consolable. Most have acquired enough clothes – even if mismatched – to cover and warm themselves. Some of the ladies of both ships are still cutting and sewing clothes made from sheets and blankets for those in need. Still, there never seem to be enough blankets on deck to warm those from the boats, especially in the intermittent fog.

The *Titanic* Survivors Committee, chaired by Margaret Brown continues in their work. Fund and subscriptions are being collected for the steerage passengers, the 'Hoffman' orphans, and the Captain and crew of the steamship. Newspaperman Carlos Hurd continues his silent battle with Rostron to get the story to the *New York World*. His self-described effort to bribe the Marconi men for writing materials has already proven unsuccessful. Captain Rostron has removed all stationery from the writing saloons, and Hurd suspects his cabin is being searched by the stewards. He and his wife talk to survivors and write their stories on scraps of writing paper he bought at the ship's store before they ran out including toilet paper and any scrap of paper they can beg, borrow or steal. Mrs. Hurd now even stays in the cabin when the stewards come in and stays the entire time they are in the cabin sitting on top of their interview notes to hide them from any searchers. Stewards and clergy continue to circulate and attempt to comfort the grieving. Rostron plans for their arrival in New York and the continuance of the original voyage. Crew members – stewards, stewardesses, cooks, bakers, butchers, and the rest – struggle under the weight of twice as many passengers as had departed from New York. Survivors express their thanks and impressions of the 'friendly and comfortable ship' to any who will listen.

'Princely treatment…They gave us practically the whole ship to ourselves…They did everything in their power for our comfort…Utmost kindness…Cannot be commended too much…The most touching care and kindness with every attention being given to all irrespective of class…All honor to them…Captain Rostron was very kind…No man could have been nobler than the Captain…He is always on duty…If he had been Captain of the *Californian*, there would have been a different story to tell…If we had had the Captain of the *Carpathia*, the *Titanic* accident would never have happened.'

A fairly accurate accounting of the living and dead of *Titanic* is emerging from the confusion of that late night. The final counts may change but a rough picture is coming into focus of the scale of the disaster. Of the 325 first-class passengers, 202 have been saved including all but 4 of the women. 118 of the 285 second-class passengers are alive and recovering about *Carpathia*. Virtually all the second-class male passengers went down with the great ship; only 14 out of 168 men lived through the night. Steerage passengers add 178 to the tally of people on *Carpathia*. 706 had departed Queenstown on April 14. Of the *Titanic* crew, 192 filled the berths on the Cunard ship out of approximately 900 who embarked on the maiden voyage. The Cunard flag flies at half-mast on *Carpathia*. Many homes near the docks in New York, Liverpool, and Southampton are dark with worry. Or mourning.

The wild changes in the weather only make it worse. Recurring fog, wind, and rain add to the somber mood. Emotions were as raw as the weather. Now *Carpathia* was coming into range. In range of deliverance for her passengers. In range of becoming visible as the most famous ship in the world. In range of communication again by her weak old Marconi set. *The New York Times, New York World, New York American, Boston Globe, New York Herald, New York Sun*, among others are all filling the air with Marconigrams clamoring for information, commissions to send the 'story', requests for famous passengers – some who had already been reported as lost on *Titanic* – to send their personal stories, and requests to put their reporters on *Carpathia* when she arrives. As if Bride and Cottam had not sent the lists of survivors out, wires came in asking for every passenger not appearing on the survivor lists. Shore stations, other ships, amateur operators; anyone with a wireless system was trying to ask their own questions and get their own answers ahead of everyone else. Cottam and Bride have already sent out between 400-500 wires with hundreds yet to go. Rostron posts a notice that the ship's Marconi men have not been occupied sending stories to the press but overwhelmed with passenger traffic to calm rumors. There has been no censorship. 'I wish to state emphatically that there have not been but 20 words sent to the press. The wireless was and is reserved for *Titanic* survivors and is 'at your service'.

She is the center of the civilized world. Reporters scramble to learn about the name *Carpathia*. The lack of information has made the appetite to know greater. *Titanic* is not just a shipwreck. It is an earth-shattering event that gives the lie to the utter faith in technology that *Titanic* symbolized. People need to know the why and the how. Thousand upon thousands are starting to gather.

Some stand on the shore and attempt to see her enter the harbor while some stand in the rain outside the Cunard and White Star offices. Others cluster near the Wanamaker store in New York City waiting for news from the roof-top Marconi station, and tens of thousands are at Pier 54 at the foot of 14th Street. Along with the throngs of people are dozens of ambulances, wagons of coffins, and lines of hearses prepared and ready for any possible needs. The news has been sketchy enough to have no solid idea what will be needed. The Cunard pier has been arranged so that passengers will just have to disembark and go to a line designated by the first letter of the last name. Customs and Immigration rules have been put aside for tonight. *Carpathia*'s past arrivals and departures had always been overshadowed by her bigger and faster competitors. Now she has met her moment and as she steams past Sandy Hook just after 6:00 p.m. on April 18, 1912. She is surrounded by a swarm of upwards of 50 tugs, launches, yachts, and other small vessels hoping to escort her towards home. Boats filled with reporters shouting through megaphones and waving fists of cash in the air to try to get on board. Captain Rostron has already decided not to subject the survivors to that trial while on his ship. "No one – repeat no one – but the harbor pilot is allowed on this ship until we dock." *Carpathia*'s crewmen are stationed along the sides of her to protect her honor and ward off any boarders. Third Officer Rees immediately pulls the ladder up after the pilot boards causing much creative language to be hurled upwards from reporters left behind. RMS *Carpathia*, the dependable and steady, is tonight the star. The Stars and Stripes is drooping wetly at her bow in the rain as she steams stolidly along - amidst all the small craft begging for her attention - and glides past the Statue of Liberty at 7:50.

Marconi New York to Operator Carpathia

Arranged for your exclusive story for dollars in four figures. Mr. Marconi agreeing. Say nothing until you see me. Meet me at Strand Hotel. Keep your mouth shut

Cunard New York to Rostron Commander Carpathia

Dilapsi bedding etc will be aesculiae aesalon relief for haaring expect sail Carper Friday afternoon how much bothroph potentibus aestuatios for dicking scenica alabado north side pier 54 Titanic marmarron membraarono tonight lower floor no omalosomes issed to herkruisen haaring priot akoluth dock petris Doctore will simply put man aboard alabado andadenoideo scenica ordenadero to dock. C.P. Sumner

Messages about payment for stories and coded transmissions set the receiving press afire as she approaches the harbor. 'Why was the news censored coming from *Carpathia*? For money? And what is the coded message that looks like gibberish? More secrets? Is there a conspiracy here? What are they hiding?' The New York press, never known for their restraint, erupts in conspiracy theories even before *Carpathia* docks. Eventually, they find out that the money was for the personal stories of Bride and Cottam and not a general account of the sinking itself. The press will be even more chagrined the long coded message turns out to be a company code for what provisions are needed to be ordered before *Carpathia* departs on her delayed voyage. Coal, herring, beef, and clean bedding were some of the secret words that had so excited the press. One news reporter does have a stunning success. The ever-industrious Carlos Hurd covers all his notes in a waterproof wrap and fills a cigar box with Champaign corks as protection against sinking. With much shouting back and forth of instructions, he throws his notes overboard to the waiting tug flying the *New York World* banner. His accounts become headlines in the late newspaper special edition.

By 8:40 p.m., Officer Bisset is supervising the lowering by davits and derrick of thirteen lifeboats at White Star Pier 59. Each white boat carries the black painted name *Titanic* on its hull. A low murmur comes from the immense crowd and photographers' flashes accompany each boat as they are lowered to the water. Slowly – frustratingly slowly to the watching crowd – *Carpathia* backs out of the White Star Pier and noses her way towards home at Pier 54. The rain has slackened to a drizzle by 9:30 p.m. when Rostron orders the gangplank lowered. She is home, and to an estimated crowd of 30,000 spectators and especially to just over 700 survivors ready to disembark, a hero.

Almost as soon as the first *Titanic* survivors disembark, the questions begin from others boarding the *Carpathia*. Marconi himself, White Star manager Franklin, various Cunard officials, newspapermen, and two United States Senators rush up the gangplank in turn. Senators Smith and Newland, of the ad hoc committee, quickly formed to investigate the disaster, seek out Ismay, Rostron, Cottam, and many others with subpoenas in their pockets to make sure witnesses do not become lost. The hearings will begin tomorrow morning at the Waldorf-Astoria.

Most of the existing *Carpathia* passengers stay aboard the ship and wonder if they will really be leaving tomorrow on their delayed voyage as promised. All *Titanic* passengers disembark except for six Chinese third-class passengers. They are held closely overnight and only released to go aboard the ship they were coming to America to work on. Due to the Chinese Exclusion Act, they are not permitted on American soil. All other passengers leave the ship. Most first and second-class passengers are met by friends or family. The third-class are assisted with clothing and money to find their own way with the help of volunteer aid workers. Nurses and doctors stand in readiness to assist. White Star representatives wait to assist and answer questions. Stretchers are stacked along the wall for any unable to make the walk. As the passengers leave the ship, they are bombarded by people asking if they know or have seen this person or that person. Grateful reunions are made next to the final extinction of hope from others knowing there are no more passengers to exit the rescue ship.

"You are a very tenacious operator, but I hardly think sending those messages now will matter Mr. Bride."

Taking off the earphones, he recognizes the person at the door and says," Hello, good to meet you, Mr. Marconi. Phillips is dead."

"I know Mr. Bride. You have done all you can. Now put those earphones away. You are done. I do have a reporter here from the *Times* who would like to speak with you and Mr. Cottam if you are able. If not, he can meet you at the Strand later."

"Yes sir. Mr. Cottam is up on deck looking for someone so I doubt if he would be available now. I know he already has his instructions to go to the Strand Hotel later and will be there, I am sure."

"That is fine. Now just send for me if I am still on board when you are done, and either I or a steward can assist you off the ship."

"Thank you, sir. I am sorry about Phillips. I did my best for him. He was a true hero."

"I know. I am sorry also, but well done to you, Phillips, and Cottam."

Up on the deck, the final *Titanic* passengers are ready to exit to solid ground again. "Mr. Cottam, I would like to thank you for your kindness to my daughter and me."

"Mrs. Hadnot, it was my pleasure. I am only sorry I was too busy to tend you both more than I did. Once again, I would like to extend my condolences about Reverend Hadnot. He was a fine man."

"Thank you. Yes, he is. Goodbye young man. I would not expect our paths to cross again since we are going to Ohio, and you are heading back to sea and England."

"Not immediately Ma'am. I have just been informed that I, along with several others from both my ship and the *Titanic* are to be detained here in New York to give testimony on what occurred. Some kind of investigation by your American Senate. I am not too clear on their authority, but we have all been ordered to cooperate and appear. I do not know as yet if it will take days, weeks, or months. But evidently, I will be staying in America for at least the immediate future and not going right back out as I had hoped on *Carpathia* tomorrow."

Elizabeth speaks up brightly, "We will be staying in New York for a short while as well until we can arrange our trip west. We are being put up at a place we have been told is right near here, the American Seamen's Friend Society on Jane Street. Maybe we can see you."

"Oh yes, that is quite close. Many seamen from the steamers stay there when in New York. It is a comfortable place – not grand or large – but comfortable. I would expect some of the other passengers and the *Titanic* officers and crew may stay there as well during the investigation, but I have not heard if that is certain or just a rumor."

"I would expect so as well. We have been told that there will be a memorial service in the main auditorium tomorrow at the hotel for all those staying there. Perhaps if you are not otherwise occupied, you could join us."

"Well, Elizabeth, I don't know any of the details regarding what I am supposed to be doing or where I will be tomorrow, but I will attend if I am able. I would like to see you again, and your mother of course."

"Come Elizabeth; let us be on our way. I am most eager to be off this ship and on solid ground again. I cannot conceive of ever going to sea again. Ever."

'Yes, Mother. I hope to see you tomorrow Harold. And if not, then very soon."

Chapter Seven

APPRECIATION AND RECRIMINATION

Sir: I beg to report that at 12:34 a.m. on the 15th inst. I was informed of urgent distress message from *Titanic*, with her position. I immediately ordered ship turned around and put in course for that position; we being then fifty-eight miles S. 42 E. from her. Had heads of all departments called and issued what I considered the necessary orders to be in preparation for any emergency.

At 2:40 a.m., saw flare half a point on the port bow, taking this for granted to be ship. Shortly after we sighted our first iceberg (I had previously had lookouts doubled, knowing that *Titanic* had struck ice, and so took every care and precaution.)

We soon found ourselves in a field of bergs, large and small, and had to alter course several times to clear bergs; weather fine and clear, light airs calm sea, beautifully clear night, though dark.

We stopped at 4 a.m., thus doing the distance in three hours and a half, picking up the first boat at 4:10 a.m.; boat in charge of an officer and he reported to me that *Titanic* had floundered. At 8:30 a.m. the last boat picked up. All survivors aboard and all boats accounted for, via fifteen lifeboats alongside (saw one bottom upward among wreckage) and according to the second officer not been launched, it having got hammed, making sixteen lifeboats and four Berthon boats accounted for.

By the time we had cleared the first boat it was breaking day, and we could distinguish the other boats all within an area of four miles. We also saw that we were surrounded by icebergs, large and small, and there miles to the N.W. of us a huge field of drift ice with large and small bergs in it, the ice field trending from N.W. round by W. and S. to S.E., as far as we could see either way.

At 8 a.m. the Leyland *S.S. Californian* came up. I gave him the principal news and asked him to search and I would proceed to New York; at 8:50 proceeded full speed. While searching over the vicinity of disaster and while we were getting people aboard I gave orders to get spare hands along and swing in all our boats, disconnect the falls and hoist up as many *Titanic* boats as possible, in our davits; also, get some on fo'castle deck by derricks. We got thirteen lifeboats, six on the forward deck and seven in davits.

After getting all survivors aboard and while searching I got a clergyman to offer a short prayer of thankfulness for those saved and also a short burial service for those lost.

Before deciding definitely where to make

for I conferred with Mr. Ismay, and though he told me to do what I thought best I informed him, taking everything into consideration, I considered New York best.

I knew we should require more provisions, clean linen, blankets, and so forth, even if we went to the Azores.

As most of the passengers saved were women and children, and they were very hysterical, and not knowing what medical attention they might require, thought it best to go to New York; also thought it would be better for Mr. Ismay to get to New York or England as soon as possible and knowing that I should be out of wireless communication with anything very soon if I proceeded to the Azores.

Again, passengers were all hysterical about ice, and pointed out to Mr. Ismay the possibility of seeing ice if we went to Halifax. Then I knew from the gravity of the disaster that it would be desirable to keep in touch with land stations all we could.

I am pleased to say that all survivors have been very plucky. The majority of women, first, second, and third classes lost their husbands, and considering all have been wonderfully well. Tuesday our doctor reported all survivors physically well.

Our first-class passengers have behaved splendidly, giving up the cabins quite voluntarily and supplying the ladies with clothes and so forth. We all turned out of our cabins to give them up to survivors, saloons, smokerooms, library and so forth also being used for sleeping accommodations. Our crew also turned out to let the crew of the *Titanic* take their quarters.

I am pleased to state that owing to preparation made for the comfort of the survivors none are the worse for exposure and so forth.

I beg specially to mention how willingly and cheerfully the whole of the ship's company have behaved throughout, receiving the highest praise from everybody, and I can assure you, that I am very proud to have such a ship's company under my command.

We have experienced very great difficulty in transmitting news, also names of survivors. Our wireless is very poor, and again, we have had so many interruptions from other ships, and also messages from shore (principally press, which we ignored). I gave instructions to send first all official messages, then survivors' private messages, and the last press messages, as I considered the first items most important and necessary.

We had haze early Tuesday morning for several hours, again more or less all Wednesday from 5:30 a.m. to 5 p.m. Strong S.S.W. winds and clear weather Tuesday with moderate rough seas.

I am Sir
Yours obediently,
A. H. Rostron
Master

Rostron has compiled his report to submit to Cunard and is preparing to testify at the Waldorf-Astoria for the American enquiry. He will give his testimony as the second witness - after Ismay - to get back to his ship and prepare for departure. Harold will testify on day one of the hearing as well. His interview with the New York Times had been published under the banner 'TITANIC'S CQD CAUGHT BY LUCKY FLUKE'. He and Bride have done their interviews and received their payments. Harold plans to put the $750 away for a possible future with a certain young lady. This morning Harold divided his clothing with Bride so he will have some decent clothing to wear when he testifies at the inquiry. He has lost all his belongings on *Titanic* and could still not get around well enough to obtain anything with the funds he received from his interview.

Carpathia is resting from her exertions along the north side of Pier 54. A line of large dray wagons is dockside filled with supplies. Starting early in the morning coal barges nuzzle against her hull and the dirty job of bunkerage begins to fill her with coal for the next adventure. Fresh linens are acquired from a fellow Cunarder docked on the other side of Pier 54. The crew is laboring hard at their tasks to get her clean, maintained, and ready to continue her interrupted voyage. Virtually all the original passengers will continue with their original plans and hope that the scheduled departure for later on the 19th will somehow be achieved. A steady stream of people visits the *Carpathia*; reporters looking for stories from *Carpathia* passengers; curiosity seekers, and not a few souvenir hunters. Crew members stand guard in the public rooms to insure that these souvenir hunters leave the cutlery, plates, and anything else with a Cunard seal on it on board the *Carpathia*. They have strict orders to make sure the hunters depart with memories and without mementos. *Carpathia* is now one of the two most famous ships in the world. One is at the bottom of the Atlantic and the newly famous is her passengers' savior.

Rostron disposes of his testimony efficiently. He gives consistent and clear explanations of his actions and with the loyalty of the fraternity of ship Captains, he refuses to criticize EJ Smith's decisions. He deals with the criticism of the lack of early communications deftly and firmly. He leaves the non-seafaring and obviously impressed Senators with little to say. An understandably nervous Harold Cottam gives his testimony often to the frustration of the Senators. The shore-bound Senators have no common frame of reference with life on board ship. Without a real knowledge of either the Marconi system he was operating or the incredible conditions existing on *Carpathia* from just after midnight on April 15, they cannot understand why he cannot give specifics on each answer. He comes across to them as short and uncommunicative. The political investigators are much more interested in finding out why more information wasn't forthcoming to the newspapers and them on the way back to New York than anything that contributed to the vast loss of life in the sinking. Numerous questions about how far he had undressed getting ready for bed before hearing the first CQD signal from T*itanic* baffle him. Repeated questions on his lack of response to an incoming Marconigram from the U.S. President and his payment by the *New York Times* for his story feel slanted to tarnish his performance and reputation. The Senators have already told him that both he and Bride will be recalled, and he dreads the thought. That means that *Carpathia* will sail without him at the key as he waits in America for what is to come.

Ismay – possibly still in shock – is a font of non-information. His testimony shows a man with little interest in the events of that night and the consequences to the passengers and employees of his White Star liner, the RMS *Titanic*. He is not a seaman, so he professes no knowledge of questions of seamanship. He is not the builder so answers all questions on the construction of the ship with a statement of no knowledge. He is not a Marconi man so has nothing to add on questions of communications. He is just the man in charge of the company – and the people in harm's way.

'I saw no passengers in sight when I entered the lifeboat.'

'I did not see what happened to the lifeboats.'

'I did not look to see after leaving the Titanic whether she broke in two.'

'I did not look to see if there was a panic.'

'After I left the bridge, I did not see the captain.'

'I saw nothing of any explosion.'

'I saw no struggle, no confusion.'

'I did not recognize any passengers on the Titanic as she sank.'

'I saw no women waiting when I entered the lifeboat.'

'I didn't see anyone in the water with a lifebelt'

'I haven't had conversation with anyone.'

Much of his testimony is summarized by a question about his knowledge of how many of the *Titanic*'s officers may have survived, to which he answers: 'I have no idea. I have not asked. Since the accident, I have made very few inquiries of any sort.'

Rostron returns to Pier 54 to finish preparations for going to sea. His clearance paperwork has been handled by local officials eager to help the hero and his provisioning is complete. The 4:00 p.m. departure of the *Carpathia* is going to occur on time. Once again, the 'Electric Spark' has made things happen. Before heading out to sea, he calls his officers and crew together and addresses them.

"Men of the *Carpathia*, I have assembled you here to show you my sincere appreciation for what you have done for me and those that you have saved. Your loyalty and obedience to every command & order have brought to you and your ship great praise. I am proud to have such men under my command. You, my men, I am proud to command. Especially must I mention the doctors, the pursers, the stewards who have done such great work in relieving the distress of the survivors. Again, I say I am proud to command such a crew. You notice at the fore, the flag – the Stars and Stripes – which we have representing the people of the United States, another flag which I now have the honor to unfurl is the blue ensign of the Royal Naval Reserve in which I have the honor to serve. The third flag, that of the Cunard Line which you have honored. I want you men to remain with this ship. Do your duty. I shall always be just with you. I shall always be fair with you. A gentleman has come aboard and laid a package in my hands saying that he wished to make some small recompense to you for all the care and consideration that you showed the survivors, that he wished the contents of the package distributed among the men of the crew. At an early date, I shall do so. Again, I wish to thank you for what you have done for me and again I say that I am proud to have such men as you serve under my command."

That afternoon Margaret Brown is back aboard her rescue ship.

She and her committee are there to see Captain Rostron. A crowd gathers on deck to hear the congratulatory speeches and witness the award presentation. Harold is just arriving back from his testimony and draws up to the back of the crowd, next to a small figure dressed in black.

"I am so glad you are here Harold. I had hoped you would be back in time. I wanted to see you before you left." Elizabeth slides her arm through Harold's and stands close to him in the cool breeze. She tightens her clasp on his arm.

"Well Elizabeth, it seems I will not be leaving right away. Bride and I were told to stand ready to come back for more testimony. My ship will leave today without me."

"I should say I am sorry, but truly I am not. I hope the hearing wasn't too unpleasant. I know you want to be done with the public foolishness. But if you are going to be here longer, well I am happy for the hearings. I can see you again then."

"Yes. I can call on you as long as we are both here, which makes losing the *Carpathia* not such a bitter pill." Harold and Elizabeth fall silent as Mrs. Brown starts to speak.

"Captain Rostron. The survivors' committee of the *Titanic* would like to present you with some tokens of our esteem and thanks for your gallant actions in saving our lives. We will do that soon as the time is short before your departure. For now, I would like to announce that we have raised just over $10,000 for assistance to destitute survivors."

After the applause dies away, the crowd exits the ship, including Elizabeth, and gathers along the quayside to watch the liner prepare to leave New York. Harold takes leave of his Captain and greets his replacement for this voyage before joining Elizabeth on shore with his gear. Exactly one week after she left New York seeking adventure and immigrants, *Carpathia* is nudged away from the dock and turns her face east once more. As she steams away - the new queen of the seas - the events and controversy around *Titanic* and the recognition of *Carpathia*'s role builds and grows on multiple continents.

In the Myrtle room of the hotel in New York City bearing the family name of one of the perished passengers – The Waldorf-Astoria – Harold testifies twice before the enquiry moves on to Washington D.C. He will testify twice more while still seeing all the sights of Washington and being wined and dined around the city. The British Board of Trade is organizing to begin their enquiry at the start of May. Both Bride and Cottam know they will be testifying there as well. Out on the cold North Atlantic swells, the CS *Mackay-Bennett* arrives on station and begins her gruesome search. She will find and recover 306 bodies. John Astor – body #124 - is identified by his clothing and jewelry. Isidor Straus - #258 - is found, but not his wife. Some say band leader Wallace Hartley will be found with his violin in a case still strapped to his body, but the *Mackay-Bennett* only notes some letters, a cigarette case, a few shillings, and a few other things. Only 56 of the 116 bodies put in canvas and buried at sea can be identified. The *Mackay-Bennett* is overwhelmed and out of supplies of coffins, embalming supplies, and canvas she carried with her. She takes 190 victims back to Halifax on her deck. Twenty-seven more bodies are found by other ships – none of them Reverend Allen Hadnot. The three long-dead occupants of the wandering and unsinkable Collapsible A are found over a month after the disaster by the liner *Oceanic*.

The next stop after the American Enquiry for Harold is home. Signing on as an operator on the *Caronia*, he returns to England and eventually Southwell. He is scheduled to testify early to a friendlier audience in Scottish Hall in Westminster. Then he can go home finally. One Marconigram sent home telling family he is ok after the *Titanic* news has been his only contact with his family. He is ready for home after the sinking, rescue, and two enquiries. He still feels bruised by his treatment in the American investigation and their conclusion that he didn't show 'proper vigilance in handling the important work confided to his care after the accident. Information concerning an accident at sea had been used by the wireless operator for his own advantage.' He rarely loses his temper, but hearing these conclusions is one instance when he does. They were not there. They are not upset about the sinking, or thankful that his work was possibly the only reason that over 700 people were saved. These politicians are upset with the perceived slight of not getting information from *Carpathia* after the wreck. Harold knows there was no order of censorship and that he didn't even know anything about the *New York Times* interview until they arrived in the harbor in New York! Their fat egos got bruised because they didn't get the information first. The fact that it was revealed that the design discussion when building *Titanic* as to how many lifeboats to carry on board took fifteen minutes but the discussion of the first cabin carpets took two hours didn't bother them, but not being able to reply to every newspaper wired question did? Well to hell with them!

 He wants to see family and friends quietly in Southwell and then return to America if possible. Elizabeth and her mother will attempt to remain in New York until they have word of the Reverend but cannot stay indefinitely. They need to get to Ohio and start their new life. Harold has staked them some funds from his *New York Times* interview to assist them while they wait, but in New York City, those funds will not last. After the rush and scrutiny of New York, Washington, and London, a quiet visit to home and hearth in Southwell is needed. Hearing rumors of a big brass-band welcome, Harold exits the train in Fiskerton and walks the five miles home alone. His now-former Captain continues on *Carpathia* and will not testify in England until June.

Restocked with supplies, full coal bunkers, and freshwater tanks, the *Carpathia* is ready to get back to her regular business. Captain and crew will try to make her interrupted voyage as normal as possible. The crew has been instructed not to discuss the previous week's events with the passengers. The passengers, by mutual consent, agree that all *Titanic* talk is now taboo. A large gala 'Grand Concert' is scheduled with singing, instrumental performances, and elaborate costumes were sewn by a ship's stewardess. Checks to the crew from the survivor's fund are to be awarded at the gala. However, from the first, all knew the next voyage will not be a normal one. She is famous now.

Crowds turn out to cheer *Carpathia* as she backs into the Hudson to leave New York and flotillas of small boats greet the Cunarder as she arrived in Gibraltar and Naples. A representative of the President of Hungary welcomes *Carpathia* and Rostron to Fiume. At each port, thousands of the curious ask to walk the decks of the '*Titanic* Rescue Ship' in wonder. Her one night's work had made her world-famous, and her Captain an international hero. Completing her delayed voyage, she stands out to sea westbound from Gibraltar on May 18, 1912, with just over 1,531 passengers en route to America. Shortly after midnight on May

29, she arrives back in New York harbor once again. Her arrival is a social and historical event, and her name is announced to the world. New York once again celebrates her and her Captain's arrival.

Almost as soon as the passengers leave the ship and step foot in America, the social whirl begins for Rostron and the crew. The Survivor's Committee boards the ship laden with awards and medals.

"Captain Rostron. The survivors' committee of the *Titanic* would like to present you with this silver loving cup. It is inscribed, 'In grateful recognition and appreciation of his heroic and efficient service in the rescue of the survivors of the Titanic on April 15, 1912.'

"This will find a place of honor on this ship, Mrs. Brown. I will share this honor with my gallant crew. We thank you, but we were only doing the duty of seamen."

Next, the entire ship's company of officers and crew assembles and are awarded – one by one – medals recognizing their actions. Gold medals are pinned on the senior officer's uniforms, silver to the junior officers, and bronze to the crew members. Harold is in England and misses the awarding of the medals. After the ceremonies are done, and the crowds have dispersed, Officer Bisset begins to go through the sacks of mail that have been sent to *Carpathia* and her Captain. Letters, gifts, proposals of marriage, and other tokens of thanks and appreciation will occupy the Captain for weeks. He also receives an invitation, along with some of his officers, to the famous Winter Garden Theater. During the performance, Al Jolson – the star of the show – stops the show and announces that there is a hero in attendance tonight and points to Rostron's theater box. With shouts and cheers, the audience rises to its feet to salute the Captain and officers of *Carpathia*. The rest of the week is rapidly filled with other salutes; each one a grand social event. Before their expected sailing on June 4, Captain Rostron, his officers, and the entire crew of the *Carpathia* have been invited to attend an event very close to his heart, a memorial band concert for the benefit of the musicians of the *Titanic*. To be held at the Moulin Rouge, formerly the New York Theatre. The bands for this gala concert will be Arthur Pryor's Band, Gustav D'Aquin's Madison Square Garden Band, Lacalle's Concert Band, New York Letter Carriers' Band, Hebrew Orphan Asylum Band, Catholic Protectory Band, Soller, and her male band, United States Army bands from the forts near New York, and United States Navy bands from the Brooklyn Navy Yard and the war vessels in port. Before sailing Rostron and Doctor McGhee plan to visit the three newly made widows that had shared his cabin after their rescue

Another wreck – this time on land - almost prevents Rostron and McGhee from their lunch with Madeline Astor, Marian Thayer, and another surviving widow Mrs. Florence Cumings. On the way to the Astor mansion, the taxi taking them from the Cunard pier loses a rear wheel and almost overturns. Shaken but intact, the good doctor and the Captain arrive outside the immense bronze entrance gates at 840 Fifth Avenue in New York. Astor, Thayer, and Cumings have already braved the ever-present swarm of news reporters and cameramen in constant attendance outside the Astor mansion. A fellow occupant of Captain Rostron's 'widows' cabin' – Eleanor Widener – has been invited but illness prevents her from attending. The Cunard officers are overwhelmed by the extravagant marble fountain in the domed entrance hall; ten feet high with spouting dolphins at its top, it dominated the glass-ceilinged room. All the ladies are still dressed in deep mourning and the huge dining room windows are still darkened in remembrance of Colonel Astor. All are similarly dressed but dealing with their grief in different ways.

Madeleine Force Astor is given a multi-million-dollar trust and the mansion on Fifth Avenue in her husband's will. That is, she will receive and be able to keep these items as long as the 18-year-old young woman remains a widow for the rest of her life. The press, which had printed her late husband's will in its entirety in the newspapers, is full of discussion of the rights and wrongs of the will and what she will do with the rest of her life. It already seemed an eternity since JJ Astor had spied the 17-year-old girl playing tennis in Bar Harbor Maine and struck up a conversation. She had not yet reached her first wedding anniversary but was already a pregnant widow subjected to a barrage of newspaper probing into her every move. She attempts to ignore the loud cries of some that Colonel Astor's death was somehow a just punishment for his divorce and quick remarriage to her. She misses her dashing husband. She even misses his favorite pet

Airedale, who also perished with him on *Titanic*.

Marian Thayer has recently been working with a spiritualist to attempt to communicate with her dead husband. He has never been found. She misses him every day. She cherishes her son John Jr. who survived with her. Recently she has been receiving letters that are growing increasingly personal, if not loving, from married Bruce Ismay. She tells the Captain of the letters but refuses to divulge the content. Rostron takes a train to visit Widow Eleanor Widener. She plans to devote her life to charitable causes. She is currently putting the finishing touches on an over three-million-dollar donation to Harvard University. She will give them a new library in honor of her lost son and husband that will also house her family's rare book collection. Rostron repeatedly expresses thanks for the thanks of the ladies and the gifts of appreciation from Mrs. Astor and the other ladies. He also speaks of his embarrassment of being suddenly thrust into the limelight after years of the quiet anonymous life as a ship's Captain. After he attends the gala band concert back in New York, he will be very glad to return to sea. One last award will be given before *Carpathia* departs; a black cat named 'Captain' to share his quarters as *Carpathia* stands out to sea on the afternoon of June 4.

Harold doesn't miss her departure by much. He is heading west on another Cunarder as the famous *Carpathia* – with her even more famous Captain - steams eastward on her regular route. Several days of testimony given in the *Titanic* enquiry followed by much welcome time at home have revived him. Mr. Marconi had given him time to decide where he wants to be posted next by allowing him to add to the staff at the Wanamaker store station in New York. Staying in New York, he could be available for almost any ship and could help with some much-needed staffing in the city. Plus, he hopes that the Hadnots are still in town, but they are gone. After news reports of the lists of recovered bodies circulated without the name of Allen Hadnot being found, they left for Ohio. Harold finds a letter waiting for him at the Marconi station, giving off the slight scent of carnations.

My Dearest Harold,

I hope you are not offended or think that I am too forward in my greeting, but that is how I feel about you. You have always thought of me as that little girl you first met in Egypt years ago. However, growing up as I have in a faraway place and under some very difficult situations has helped me very early on to know what I want and what is important. I am no longer a little girl and know that you are very important to me.

Mother and I left for Ohio once the final list of recovered people from the Titanic was posted, and

Father's name was not listed. I still worry about my Mother, but I think she has realized that Father is lost. She speaks of no more trips across the ocean, and how she always had a feeling about the Titanic. I am not sure that she will travel anywhere again once we arrive in Ohio. I fear for her mind at times but hope and pray she takes comfort in her faith as I do.

So now we head to the farm, and I can learn about growing sugar beets, corn, tomatoes, etc. I am not sure what my role at the farm will be, or what it will be like learning a new family. I will post a letter to you at the Marconi station as soon as I have my own postal information to include. I know you mentioned that you might be staying in New York and working either in the city or looking for new locations for shore stations. I hope that my letter will reach you quickly. Now, as to the future, Mr. Cottam, I have found out that we have extended family on a small farm somewhere on Long Island so there is a possibility of me spending time there. Again, forgive me for being so forward and not lady-like. However, my life in India and the experience on Titanic have made me realize that not a moment should be wasted on pretension or conventions. Also, I remember your words about using the funds from the New York Times interview as our start and assume you were not teasing me.

Love,

Elizabeth

Ps - I heard your Captain Rostron speak before we left and he mentioned you very prominently. He said, 'I must mention the wireless operator, through his attention to duty, and his interest in his work, that I am indebted for the opportunity to do something really useful.' I was and am very proud of you.

Carpathia happily returns to her regular routes from New York to the Mediterranean, and back to being an anonymous and comfortable friend. Rostron uses every spare minute on board opening packages, parcels, and letters from admiring people across the world. He tries to answer each letter, open each package, and turn down each marriage proposal. July 1 in Naples, he will leave the *Carpathia* and travel overland back towards home for the British Enquiry and rest at home. The black cat 'Captain' remains with the ship, along with her other awards. *Carpathia* has a new Marconi man as Harold remains in New York after his return from England. He works at the downtown Marconi station atop the huge Wanamaker Store and writes long letters to Elizabeth in Ohio. William 'Sailor Bill' Prothero takes over as the new Captain of *Carpathia*. The *Titanic* survivors and *Carpathia* witnesses are left to process the events in their own way. Some will revel in their new lives and live to tell the stories over and over, often with wider and wider exaggerations. Some will closet themselves away – like Ismay – and consider their lives ruined by the sinking. Some like Captain Lord of the *Californian* will be forever under a cloud. He will lose his position with Leyland lines and find a new job commanding nitrate freighters in South America. He will spend all of his spare moments protesting how he is portrayed. For some, their involvement will determine the success or failure of their careers. None of the surviving *Titanic* officers will ever achieve command. Some – like Harold and Elizabeth – will move on to new lives and possibilities even as the world stumbles blindly towards war.

Chapter Eight

THE GATHERING STORM

She rests along the sunny shores of the Adriatic in Fiume during the last golden days of peace for most of the world. Close to fifty nations will soon be at war. Over 65 million men will be mobilized for war and 37 million of those will become casualties over the next four years. More than a hundred ships at least as large as *Carpathia* will be sunk by torpedoes, mines, and surface fighting during the war, including several involved with *Titanic*. Her sister ship *Britannic* – converted to a hospital ship – will be sunk by a mine. The much-maligned *Californian* is torpedoed and will join *Titanic* which she ignored at the bottom of the sea.

The world – and the *Carpathia* – is moving on. Captain Rostron leaves the *Carpathia* for good. He travels to the United States where President Taft presents him a Congressional Gold Medal in the East Room for his work with the rescue. James Bisset leaves the *Carpathia* for military training and future promotion; filing away his notes listing some of the 'what ifs' on *Titanic* that he hopes to write in his memoirs one day.

If the ship had been built with a double hull, a glancing blow would not have sunk her.

If she had kept full speed instead of full astern, she might have swung around the berg.

If she had searchlights, she might have been able to spot the berg and avoid it.

If she had extra lookouts, she might have seen the berg in time to avoid.

If she had a bigger rudder, she might have turned more quickly.

If her bulkheads extended up to the deck heads, she would have stayed afloat longer.

If she had started signaling to Californian sooner, they might have seen her.

If Californian had two radio operators, they would have heard her distress signals.

If she had more lifeboats, more could have been saved.

If there had been a lifeboat drill on Titanic, more would have been saved.

If there hadn't been the giant conceit of 'unsinkable' more might have been saved.

William 'Sailor Bill' Prothero is the new master of *Carpathia*. A staunchly patriotic Britisher and Church of England member, he will be the longest-serving master of *Carpathia*. His luxuriant black mustache and heavy beard identify him from a distance as he walks the decks. He is a popular Captain, and his smile is often seen separating the mass of facial hair. Even after being stranded in what he describes as a hurricane – with broken steering gear and waves breaking over the rails – no fault is ascribed to the popular Captain. At the outbreak of war, *Carpathia* scurries off to Naples where she once again takes on frightened passengers. Lines of Americans and others waited at Cunard trying to book passage on the famous ship hope to escape to America on her first war-time trip across the Atlantic.

Leaving Naples in a pre-dawn fog, several passengers gather at the rail pointing into the gloom. Joining them at the rail Prothero easily makes out the dim shape drawing their attention, a German surface raider. Behind him, he hears the clanging of rushed steps on the metal ladder from the bridge. Holding up his hand, the Captain forestalls his watch officer from speaking and simply says, "I've seen it".

Once again *Carpathia* is called upon to charge into the dark at her maximum speed. After sending out a message about the danger and *Carpathia*'s course, the good news of another ship relaying her information via wireless is given to the Captain. Knowing that the surface raider will have heard the broadcast course and speed and move to that course, the Captain quickly orders a course change Northwest. "Full speed ahead. Put the coal to her." The German surface raider is never seen again and *Carpathia* steams safely westward through the fog.

Now her unglamorous wartime work begins. The distinctive red and black Cunard livery is repainted a dull wartime grey. Besides carrying fleeing Europeans to safety, she carries vital materials needed for the war-torn continent. Cotton, lubricating oil, tin, wheat, sugar, flour, bacon, and automobiles, and even crated airplanes fill her holds and line her decks. On one trip she carries $25 million in securities from the Bank of England. She is one of the double-bottomed Cunarders deemed safe enough to carry two thousand tons of oil on every voyage to keep the oil-starved Allies going. She will carry all she can take through the dangerous waters to Europe to supply those in need during wartime. In May of 1915, *Carpathia* undergoes another metamorphosis as she becomes a 'trooper'.

First to arrive are the Canadians. Bound for Quebec, they take the cars across their vast country from the rugged western reaches of Canada. The 27th and 31st Battalions ride the Canadian Northern and Canadian Pacific Railroads for their days-long trip to meet *Carpathia*. Joining them are the headquarters staff of the Brigade they will join – the Sixth Canadian Brigade. Young soldiers from the prairies near the Red River Valley of Winnipeg and surrounding Calgary, Alberta mix with backwoods and mountain men from deep in the rugged Rockies. They talk about their first visit to the wonders of a big city like Quebec and what awaits them overseas in France. What will the food be like? What are French women really like? Crowds greet them with cheers and gifts at every stopover along the way. Perhaps wisely, the big city visits anticipated by the young soldiers are limited to views out the train windows with no freedom to roam the city. Or to get into trouble.

Boarding the famous liner, the wide-eyed young men are directed towards their berths before being released to wander the Cunarder. They deposit their 'vessel on which I sailed has arrived safely overseas' cards for their families in the appointed sacks around the ship. They will be mailed when and if the ship arrives unharmed in England. Many seek out *Carpathia* crew members to see if they had been part of the *Titanic* rescue experience. The Calgarians are interested to a man in seeking out any with knowledge of Calgary residents and *Titanic* first-class passengers Albert and Vera Dick. Their story has always been much talked about all through Alberta province. The Dicks were not just famous in Calgary for their wealth from business and real estate success. The story of their time on the *Titanic* had caused many hours of conversation and gossip in all levels of Alberta society. The young bride on her extended honeymoon to the Holy Land and through the grand tour of Europe. The infatuation of a young ship's steward with Vera during the voyage and her scandalous flirting with him while on her honeymoon with her new husband. Their friendship with doomed *Titanic* designer Thomas Andrews on board ship. The varying stories of their securing places in Lifeboat 3 promoting much soft whispering of gossip in many drawing rooms across the province. Were they locked in a final embrace when a ship's officer pushed them both into the boat? Did Albert sneak into the boat dressed as a woman? Gossips always had full and exact details to expound on with great confidence in all scenarios.

As *Carpathia* departs for her two day steam up the St. Lawrence from Quebec to enter the Atlantic, the packed-in soldiers get a glimpse of how their 'leisurely' voyage will be organized: four shifts for breakfast and tea, daily inspections, and boat drills, classes in guard mounting, camp duties and cooking, field defenses, map reading, general parades on deck, exercises, and classes specific to each of the different detachments. The crowded soldiers react to their conditions as soldiers everywhere do. Some find little to complain about and some discover nothing to their liking, especially the food.

'This old boat isn't a palace but believe me is very comfortable. The crowd is very fine.'

'We have had one meal already and if they are all as good, I will be quite satisfied.'

'Our quarters are excellent.'

'A lovely voyage, the weather was ideal.'

'The Carpathia is not a racehorse by any means, but it is very steady.'

'We are packed in like sardines.'

'" By no means, a pleasant voyage.'

"Vile, crowded and filthy.'

'The food would make you sick and would have caused a riot in a logging camp.'

She steams unescorted at first, relying on stealth and a faster speed than any U-Boat to reach England safely. Nearing the English coast, sharpshooters and machine guns from each Battalion are placed on deck as a defense against submarines in those early innocent days of the war. Men are forbidden to smoke on the deck, and she runs with no lights at night. After the United States enters the war, she still departs from her familiar New York pier, but the vast numbers of soldiers departing for Europe are to be funneled through tiny Hoboken, New Jersey. Ferries will take thousands of the new doughboys from the newly appropriated German steamship docks across to the waiting *Carpathia* and other liners. As the scale of the shipments across the Atlantic blossoms, she has to learn how to convoy. Grouped with other liners and protected by voyagers, destroyers, and submarine chasers, the great convoys full of troops and supplies make their ponderous way across the Atlantic, where the feared U-Boats live. She eagerly welcomes the sight of the Azalea-class British sloops, and American Wickes-class American destroyers like the U.S.S *Lea* as they steam into view to protect their charges from the dreaded torpedoes of Germany. Thousands more American soldiers including the engineers of the 330th, 314th, and the 10th Forestry engineers call *Carpathia* home for their entry into the war zone. On some trips, she sails alone at her top speed to Halifax and there waits for other ships to form a convoy. Then she crawls along at the speed of the slowest ship of the convoy. But she doesn't mind. After all, she is the 'comfortable' one and not a racehorse. Back and forth she steams carrying troops and the stuff of war to keep the Allies supplied. Slow, tense convoy moments intersperse with the grinding boredom of sitting becalmed in Halifax harbor waiting for others to join her trip. The welcome sight of escorts steaming into sight and the sight of land once again after another trip through torpedo water is always a cause for celebration. Trip after trip she does her duty silently. She is no longer the most famous ship afloat.

Harold Cottam has remained in touch with the ship that briefly made him famous. His sleepless nights on *Carpathia* in April 1912 have afforded him some financial security due to his *New York Times* interview - unusual in a man of formally limited means and age. It has also given him an elevated status among his community of Marconi men and men in the steamship industry generally. Now in the vast expansion of the Marconi enterprises caused by the Great War, he is considered an 'old man'. A pioneer. When he stops in the first-floor office of the mammoth Wanamaker store or Marconi headquarters to check for his mail or to review the wireless traffic from ships at sea, the young clerks jump to meet his needs and answer his questions. When taking the steamboat *Shinnecock* from Pier 13 to Long Island for his Marconi duties, he is always told that his money is not welcome and is allowed on board for free. For now, the boy from the English countryside is enjoying the vibrant life of New York City. He had recently walked down Broadway from the Wanamaker Store – past Astor Place and the terminus of the world-famous Brooklyn Bridge to the end of Manhattan at Battery Park. There in the shadow of Castle Clinton, Harold viewed the new Wireless Operator's Memorial. Carved into the granite monument are the words, 'Elevated in memory of wireless operators lost at sea at the post of duty'. Near the bottom of the first column of the plaque is the name of his friend Jack Phillips. Like Reverend Hadnot, Jack's body was never found. New York teems with memories of the *Titanic*; from the grand Cunard and White Star offices, Piers 54 and 59 themselves, to the Straus memorial to the red brick home of the American Seamen's Friend Society Sailor's Home and Institute where some *Titanic* survivors were housed. Sometimes, even now amid war, the controversy of *Titanic* would be in the newspapers again. Some event would be in the news that could be related to some small bit of testimony during the enquiry. Or some news of a survivor's life or death would appear. The news that the discussion of the style and colors of *Titanic*'s first-class cabin carpets occupied Ismay and his company for two hours while the discussion of the number of lifeboats took a mere fifteen minutes was featured as a recurring front-page story from time to time. Harold's former Captain Rostron's demand to have all his records made public to show there was no censorship to the public of the sinking news had very little mention by those same newspapers. That was not big news and would make no interesting headlines. Every time some *Titanic* news would splash across the headlines, Harold would think of Elizabeth. Should I tell her this in my next letter?

Her last carnation-scented letter had been filled with talk of the farm and her hopeful plans for the near future. A recent move to a new farm outside of Napoleon, Ohio had moved her family out of kerosene lighting and one first floor stove to a new farm with electric lighting and more heat for the winter months. She seemed very excited to finally have comforts above what she had in the Indian mission all those years ago. She would write in terms of moving up to a level of comfort she had on *Carpathia*, but not to the extent she experienced on *Titanic* yet. She rarely mentioned the *Titanic* except for brief references to her mother's erratic behavior or a rare dream of her own. When a survivor would be in the news she would write about it briefly, but most of her letters were about her daily life. She spoke of the two Lutheran congregations near her; one English-speaking and the other speaking only German. She and her mother were welcomed in the English language church, but even with their missionary background, a distance between organized churches and themselves had arisen. Elizabeth only wrote of it in one past letter, but she felt at times that she had lost both her father and mother to organized religion. They had given their all to the mission and their faith and now both were lost one way or another. Other letters spoke of getting a new Ford Ferguson tractor, the results of various plantings of corn, sugar beets, grains tomatoes, and the daily efforts of planting and harvesting. The special Christmas bag that she helped assemble for the children in church on Christmas with special hard-to-find treats was always a highlight as was the occasional nickel given to each for ice cream in town. The little facets of her daily life didn't appear in her latest letter. She was focused on the future. And her Harold.

My Dearest Harold,

How I miss you. That will change though as I believe the plans are now set finally. We heard from Mr. Stegkamper's family yesterday and the answer is yes. They will be happy to have me for a visit or the entire summer at their farm on Long Island. I will not know the length of time I can stay at the outset of the trip. I will have to keep in contact with those here at home to see how Mother is and if I am needed. She says repeatedly that I should go and not worry about her, but you know how fragile a state she lives in physically and spiritually. The Stegkamper family farm is in Easthampton, which is one of the places you indicated, would be well for steamboat access and generally close to most things. They said their farm is near the Mulford Farm, which is a pre-revolutionary war farm. It sounds like the farm is mostly a dairy farm. I am also given to understand that it is also near some of the so-called cottages of the very rich, but if I don't have to see more of those 'first-class Titanic passenger' types too often, that will be just fine with me. I only want to see you again. I don't know how close it is to those secret places you told me you travel to looking for more Marconi locations, but I feel it must be close enough. So, very soon my love, we will be together again.

I do not much like the idea of leaving and making extra work for those here this summer. Working both the corn - and the stacking of the shocks later in the summer - and the everlasting harvesting of those five acres of tomatoes is hard enough with a full crew of harvesters. Still, Mother assures me that she has the extra help she needs. She tells me, again and again, I should go and that my future is not here on the farm, but where my heart is. And that place is with you.

I assume that you are still at the main office and will send this letter there. In further letters, if the address is different from Marconi Wireless Company of America, 233 Broadway, New York, please inform me in your next letter. I will be eager to hear about your work situation. I have heard grand things about the Woolworth Building - the tallest building in the world - where the main office is located.

My love, I must close this letter as I hear Mother calling me to chores. I will count the days until we can be together again. I think often of how blessed I am to be alive. Without you, and your ship Carpathia, I would not be alive to love you at all. I thank God every day that he put you in Titanic's and my path. You have saved me in every way.

I cherish you and each of your letters. I am counting the days.

Elizabeth,

The war at sea takes a deadly turn as Germany announces a move to unrestricted submarine warfare. Now there are no longer any ships considered neutral. No American or other supposed neutral in the war flag will protect a ship as it did in the early days of the war. Everyone everywhere is now fair game for the lancing death of the German torpedoes. The great Cunarder *Lusitania* succumbs to a torpedo in May 1915 and speeds the American entry into the war. She takes over 1,100 souls to the bottom with her. 1,410 ships would go down in 1916 and over 3,000 ships would be sunk in 1917. Hospital ships are now targeted as well. The vast Atlantic Ocean is a killing ground.

My only Harold,

I am glad you are enjoying some of the parts of your New York experience. Your description of the marble floors and luxurious appointments you see in the Woolworth Building sound beautiful. Yes, I am glad you found time to attend a concert in the auditorium in the Wanamaker annex. How many stores in the world contain an auditorium for 1,300 people and an organ with chimes, snare drums, kettle drums, and cymbals? No wonder you were amazed! Just walking in and out of a store that has a restaurant that seats over 1,000 people would be amazing for this farm girl. What a contrast! My quiet life amongst the prairies of western Ohio is very different than what you are experiencing now. Still, I detect in your letters a longing for both England and the simpler life.

I am glad to hear that you are treated like a hero on the steamboats to Long Island when you travel for work. You certainly saved me and have always been a hero to me. I do think that it is justified that they extend extra courtesies to you as part of that wireless man community. I am sure you would do the same to them. In addition, not having to pay for your passage is welcome always.

Please do not continue to worry about the difference between the Anglican and Lutheran denominations. I even had a long talk with Mother - on one of her good days - about this and she agrees. Both faiths basically believe in the creeds, the nature of Christ, and the resurrection. They share so many of the same beliefs that the distinction between Protestant and reformed Catholic is merely a matter of a label. To me, this certainly will not be a barrier between us.

Even in the midst of all the war news, I have seen a

few stories recently regarding Titanic survivors. I try not to take much notice, but the ever-growing nature of the heroism they say they exhibited that night sickens me. I was there. But I will not discuss it more. I have no wish to relive that night again, and yes in answer to your question, the dreams come much less frequently now.

I am still counting the days until we are together again. Once we know if you will have to go to England for work and also how I can arrange travel to New York and beyond, if necessary, we can make firm plans.

Mother sends her love. (Yes really!) As I do in my thoughts and prayers. Please be careful in your work *and pray we can be together soon.*

Love,

Elizabeth

The Great War swirls around *Carpathia* and her famous former Captain. She makes one dangerous transit of the U-Boat-infested Atlantic after another carrying the men and materials of war to the European Allies. On December 6, 1917, *Carpathia* and current Captain Prothero are at sea and not in the familiar harbor at Halifax where they often wait for convoys to assemble. That morning an inconsequential low-speed collision occurs between a French cargo ship and the Norwegian ship S.S. *Imo*. The collision jars barrels of highly flammable benzol on her decks and she begins to burn. Evacuated and alone, she drifts to shore where only minutes later, she - and the tons of munitions she is carrying to the war zone – vanish in the largest man-made explosion recorded on earth until that time. The one-knot collision's toll is over 2,000 dead and 9,000 more wounded by the explosion, fire, shattered flying glass, and collapsing buildings. Vaporized water briefly exposes the harbor bottom and then is replaced by a tsunami that obliterates a small First Nations settlement and its inhabitants. Once again, a wireless man – in the traditions of Jack Binns, Jack Phillips, and Harold Cottam - saves further casualties. Patrick Coleman and his Marconi set are stationed at the local rail yard and learn of the dangerous cargo on the ship before it explodes. He quickly sends out urgent wireless messages to stop an incoming train.

'Hold up the train. Ammunition ship afire in harbor and will

explode. Guess this will be my last message. Goodbye boys.'

Patrick Coleman does not survive.

Captain Rostron, commanding ships like *Carmania* and the famous flyer *Mauretania*, continues to be known as a lucky commander. Sailors always seek a berth on a ship with a Captain known as lucky. Ever since avoiding all the surrounding ice on *Carpathia*'s dash to the *Titanic*, he has led a charmed life. His previous commands are disappearing from the seas during the war one after another. The *Lusitania* goes down in 1915, as does the *Veria*. *Alaunia* and *Ivernia* succumb to hostile action and rest on the bottom as does the *Andania*. Six of his previous commands now lay quietly below the sea; all sunk after he leaves those ships.

Harold continues to work on both sides of the Atlantic throughout the war. Scouting the Long Island area, he assists in setting up additional wireless stations on the wind-swept island in cooperation with the military. Taking ship to England he helps develop more stations to assist the convoys and begins the secret work of ways to monitor the wireless communications of England's enemies. Without knowing whether Harold is in New York, Long Island, or on another continent Elizabeth continues her faithful letter writing.

My Dearest Darling,

Yes, I agree. You have certainly been working with all your might and main. From being able to arrange your tender proposal of marriage on the wind-swept dunes of Montauk even though it was closed by the military to all inhabitants, to this new plan; your efforts are quite breathtaking. Now I don't really believe that you arranged for the dirigible from the Air station to circle over us while you spoke your tender proposal of marriage, I would not be at all surprised if you had made it happen somehow. I do question though if you arranged for the dirigible, how you could not find a better conveyance out to the end of the island than that broken-down old buckboard to get us there. My teeth are still chattering from the bouncing and shaking!

No, I don't think we are moving too fast as my mother says. She does not realize that I have loved you ever since that chance meeting in Venice those many years ago. And in these uncertain times - and with my past Titanic experiences in mind - I think we must move forward with haste since the future is never guaranteed. Even with the risks of wartime ship voyages must be taken. When I saw you again on the Carpathia, I knew that you were my savior in more ways than one. My Father and I even discussed it. I am quite confident my Father would approve if he were still with us as he always saw me - even when I was very young - as more grown-up than my mother ever has to this day.

I think that it is very exciting that you met Thomas Edison! He and Mr. Marconi seem to be everywhere and into everything all the time. I am surprised that you were allowed to meet him while he was viewing torpedo tests in Sag Harbor. I would think they would have kept everyone away. And yes, I agree with you about Mr. Marconi. He must be the first person to be an Honorary Knight of the Victorian Order in England, a Captain in the Italian Army, and an officer in the Italian Navy. Plus, he is a Senator in the Italian Senate. He also must be as rich as Croesus with the news I saw that our Navy has ordered 10,000 wireless sets from him. I am most grateful to him that he will consider chaperoning my trip to you if you remain in England. I pray that it will work out.

Now, my love, I must close. Before I do, I almost forgot to tell you again that I have no objection to the use of the Church of England wedding service. I am sure that Captain Prothero will do an exemplary job and I will be very thankful to him to assist us in joining as man and wife on board ship.

All my love,

Elizabeth

Once again Harold will walk the welcoming decks of *Carpathia*. Being transferred for an uncertain length of time to England and Scotland, he will miss both the frenzy of New York City and the peace of Long Island. He does not see the start of the construction of the new Cunard office. He had gaped in awe at the plans for a headquarters for Cunard that he can only compare to the pictures he had seen of the ancient Roman baths. A soaring 60′ tall lobby lit with skylights, marble and carved stone, and murals wherever one looks; it was going to be all gilt and grandeur. He will miss his trips to Long Island. The route through the Long Island Sound, through Plum Gut into Gardiner's Bay to Sag Harbor, and the long wharf were as familiar as his route to the Wanamaker store in the city. His travel on Long Island past the Shinnecock Golf Club to Westhampton and then back east to the Sagaponek and Amagansett Marconi stations and then onwards to Montauk are now to be part of his history – at least for now. He has always appreciated the special treatment and attention from the Montauk Steamship Company's captains, ticket sellers, and wireless men - all the while craving solitude for the trip. He welcomes the opportunity to travel to his new posting on *Carpathia*. She is an old friend. A ship that is still 'friendly and comfortable'. His memories were a jumble of stress, no sleep, tension, and sadness. And of her. He has not been aboard since 1912, and he finds little changed. Updated and more powerful Marconi equipment now fill his familiar workstation on the aft boat deck. The Marconi man on board is surprised at the ordinary appearance of the man who is legendary throughout the wireless society. Captain Prothero looks decidedly odd to Harold as he can only envision the ship's bridge with the figure of Rostron walking from wing to wing. He does find the Captain engaging and open to his requests and suggestions for his plans for the future.

Guglielmo Marconi has agreed to be part of those plans as well. Contacted – by wireless of course – by the young man who has brought his wireless invention into wide acceptance, he finds time to help. As part of the Italian delegation to the United States after Austria's collapse, he is going to be in talks about the completion of the war against Germany and the post-war world for Italy. When he returns to Italy, he agrees to chaperone Elizabeth who will be waiting impatiently in New York to cross the Atlantic.

All is arranged. The plans are made. Elizabeth says her goodbyes to her terrified Mother in Ohio. She begs and pleads with her daughter not to chance her life again on an Atlantic voyage. Especially in wartime. But her mind and heart are set. Harold awaits a Marconigram telling him of her arrival in England. Still a bit unsure of the length of time he will be posted to England, he pushes ahead with the plans, nevertheless. After all, it is wartime. No time to waste. Once the two lovers are together at last in the same country, they can make their final plans. At that point after all, what can go wrong? In wartime. On an Atlantic voyage.

Chapter Nine

WORLD AT WAR

The entire world seems to be dissolving. Death is everywhere in 1918. Suffocating smells of cordite and black smoke float over the high seas to mark the graves of sunken ships. Damp and reeking odors of blasted trenches rise into the air where the great armies squat amidst the wreckage tell of the death underfoot on the battlefields. Fever smells of the sickroom fill the hospitals, ships, and homes across the world. The jagged edges and contradictions of all the new technologies and the faith in those technologies are visible everywhere. The *Titanic* was the largest man-made moving object in the world at the time and thought to be unsinkable. Those new technologies of the time didn't save it. It now lies two miles down in the North Atlantic. New technologies have produced weapons of such efficiency that tens of thousands of young men can be killed in a single day during World War One – the war to end all wars. Yet, new methods and medicines cannot prevent the same number of people from dying on a single day from the worldwide flu pandemic. More people will die of influenza in one year than in the four years of the Black Death Bubonic Plague from 1347-1351. Its effect is so devastating that the average life span in the United States is depressed by 10 years. Before the Great Flu Pandemic of 1918 mysteriously disappears, deaths are estimated from 20-40 million people worldwide. By

1918, when the pandemic grabs hold of the world, most of the major bloodletting of the war has already occurred. The major land battles have a staggering cost in lives and generate the headlines but across most of the world's surface, people were dying every day. No big headlines. Just mourners.

Land Battles in Europe		Ships sunk at Sea	
Passchendale	850,000 casualties	1916	1,516
Gallipoli	500,000 casualties	1917	3,723
Verdun	975,000 casualties	1918	145 per month
Somme	1,200,000 casualties	Hospital Ships	16

Captain Rostron watches the futile struggle at Gallipoli where almost 400,000 young men are wounded or killed, from offshore in command of the *Almunia*. His charmed life continues as the *Almunia* is one of the 20 out of the total 25 ship Cunard fleet that would be sunk during hostilities. But once again, only after he departs for another new command.

Kapitänleutnant Wilhelm Werner has made many departures during the war and countless more since he was a young man just entering the German U-Boat service years ago. Now he is preparing to depart on his third war patrol of 1918. He claimed 7 ships on his patrol ending January 23, 1918, including the hospital ship *Rewa* and avoids being hit by the attacking British submarine E-51. His month-long patrol from February to March gives him 8 more ships sunk and the unexploded torpedo strike on the hospital ship *Guildford Castle*. He has accomplished the goal that he mentioned in the peaceful pre-war atmosphere of Cafe´ Florian. He has made his mark. He has succeeded and been promoted as a U-Boat commander with over 60 Allied ships sent to the bottom. The idealistic young man from Venice of years ago is long gone. He is now a deadly efficient and ruthless wartime commander. He has successfully directed his Type 51 U-Boat in attacks and avoided several of His Majesty's submarines. A hospital ship's broad green stripe circling the hull and bright red crosses painted on the sides do not deter him from firing his deadly torpedoes. Twice he has sunk British ships and brought survivors on board the rolling decks of U-55 only to submerge underneath those survivors leaving them to founder and drown. He has been decorated with the Iron Cross second and first-class and the Royal House Order of Hohenzollern. He is determined to have the Pour le Mérite – The Blue Max – hanging from his neck before the summer is out. He can visualize himself wearing his country's highest decoration when he gets his next home leave, whenever that might be. Rested and supplied for another long patrol, the U-55 slides quietly into the choppy English Channel on his way to the North Atlantic hunting grounds for a new war patrol in early July 1918.

Preparations for departure on the *Caserta* are well underway before Guglielmo Marconi and Elizabeth Hadnot arrive. Half the tonnage of the *Carpathia*, she is a lonely-looking thing. Named after the city of the same name, she had been given few of the attributes of the beautiful Italian region of Campania when she had been built and the years have not been kind to her since. She has been called a 'cattle boat' without a trace of irony. She is anonymous and unnoticed. Just another small steamer plying her trade. She will travel in convoy with USS *Covington,* USS *DeKalb,* and several other American, British, and Italian ships full of American troops for the continent protected by the American ship *Frederick.* Marconi has chosen her from a small selection of Italian ships still making the Atlantic crossing and also to keep his name out of the papers – and away from German U-Boat interest. Only the Captain has been told of his real identity. To all others, he introduces himself simply as Miss Hadnot's uncle Antonio. Their accommodations can be described as austere at best. They will have to transship to another vessel after landing at Brest, France to get to England and Italy, respectively. All the conveniences of a more comfortable voyage just are impossible to arrange in wartime, but they will both be completely satisfied if they simply complete a safe passage in convoy O.S. 35.

Elizabeth cuts quite a swath on *Caserta*. With her flashing smile, striking blue eyes, and the added status of being one of the few women on board, she is the object of much attention from most of the 47th Division crammed below decks. The eager Doughboys quickly find out that smiles and a kind word are all that they will receive from her. Stories of their homes along with wild tales – true and exaggerated – of the U-Boat encounters are the talk along the rusting ship's rails as they try to impress her. Many stand and watch critically as the two small guns mounted on *Caserta* thunder in their daily gunnery practice. The constant activity of a ship at sea in wartime is endlessly fascinating to the becalmed Army soldiers and helps to pass the days. Drills, shouted orders, and the constant signaling and maneuvering are a complete mystery to the landsmen. When signalmen like MJ McNamara on *DeKalb* wave and waggle towards *Caserta*, the soldiers try to decipher the strange language with little success. Still, the *DeKalb* has a good reputation, no matter the strange language she speaks with her flags. She has carried more than 10,000 United States troops to Europe on her voyages so far. She is known as a smart ship. So, when on the second day out, her twin funnels send out billows of smoke and signalman McNamara waggles his flags furiously, she gets an immediate reaction. German 'pipe' has been sighted! A long white trail of bubbles streaks by the *Caserta* and explodes against *Covington* with a roar. She immediately lists to port and begins to lower her lifeboats.

"That must be the U-86! Look at the way she sails right through the convoy! What brass! If that is the '86, it would be the same damnable Captain Patzig that sunk the *Llandovery Castle*. She was a marked hospital ship too! Then the sod rammed her lifeboats and gunned down the people in the water! I hope someone sinks that bastard!"

The anonymous soldier walks away trailing a truly creative stream of profanity leaving Elizabeth standing alone on deck. Despite her fear, she cannot look away. The submarine slides evilly back underwater in the distance before the *Frederick* can engage her. *Convington* moans and heels further over and is abandoned after her wounding. She will be gone when the convoy docks at Brest the next day.

Finally reaching her final destination at Liverpool, Elizabeth sees her. There she is! How much more massive she looks now with her soaring steel walls studded with sturdy rivets. Her distinctive coloring is covered in somber war-time grey, but her personality still peaks out from each porthole. For Elizabeth, each impression is as clear as if after a summer rain. The incredible length of *Carpathia* after the much smaller cross-channel ferry. The shrieking whistles and clanging machinery of the Liverpool harbor. The first time Elizabeth had seen her, everything was such a blur. Now it is all so real. Now she holds an exciting future and purpose. She is their touchstone – their reason for being. And being together. Now she is here with her solid deck underfoot. Harold will arrive sometime later this hot July day from London. They are due to depart around 8:00 a.m. on the 15th. and to be married the next day. Mr. Marconi – with his trademark florid Italian gallantry - had left her in Brest. After a drenching, tumbling wet trip across the Channel in a small steamer, she is grateful for the solid feeling under her feet and her first glimpse of her fiancé in months. Captain Prothero has been solicitous of her request to be informed of the arrival of her fiancé and excited for the wedding, almost like a surrogate father. In the short time she has been aboard she has seen the big Welshman smile tenderly at her when he thinks she does not see. Her first target on deck had been visiting the small Marconi house on the raised boat deck. Memories wash over her as she greets Marconi operator Hugh Francis and sees the familiar space. He gives her a polite greeting before breaking into a large grin almost hidden under his huge drooping mustache as someone steps out of the small bunk area.

"Hello, Miss Hadnot."

"Oh, my heaven! Harold, my darling!" She hurtles into his arms like a carnation-scented bullet. "Why didn't you tell me you were here? When did you get here? Is everything all right? Don't you ever surprise me like this again. Oh, how I love you."

The Marconi operator grins, winks, and walks away as the young couple embrace near the lifeboats.

"I was able to get away early and Captain Prothero was nice enough to assist me in my surprise attempt. I have been here since yesterday and have been counting the minutes until you arrive."

"You mean you have been here safely on board while I was being tossed about coming across the channel?"

"Yes, Dear."

"Oh, you are an evil man Mr. Cottam. But I am dreadfully happy to see you. It was an awful trip from France. The Captain of that vessel wanted to get across that Channel as fast as possible – weather and waves be damned. Still, I did have the honor to meet a wonderful fellow passenger on the hell-ship. He is a Canadian chaplain coming from Brest. He is here on *Carpathia* as well. After being grievously wounded in France he is going home to recuperate. His name is Chaplain Webster Harris, and he is a brave and good man. But don't be jealous. I told him all about you. Plus, he is happily married and a man of the cloth. He is paralyzed and in a chair from his wounds. He was conducting a burial service on the front lines when he was wounded by shrapnel. Now he is on his way home to Alberta and the church he left there. He is looking forward to meeting you."

"I will be honored to meet him, my love. Now let me help you get settled. The Captain has made sure our cabins are perfect. He did tell me that this voyage might be slower than usual however what with the speed of some of the ships listed in our convoy and the zigzagging and all. I told him that since this was our wedding trip, we are in no hurry. Just keep the U-Boats away from us and he can make the trip as long as he needs to."

Preparations are being made everywhere. Ships' crews labor in the dank heat to ready their ships to depart. Captains confer and discuss the latest U-boat sightings, rumors, and sinkings. Many ships are sought out by the dreaded German submarines on the outward leg of their trips even though inbound ships filled with supplies and American troops are more highly prized targets. Navigators study their charts and ready for the strain of keeping the 17 ships of Convoy O.L. 24 together. The convoy is being made up of two groups. O.E. 18 on its way to the Mediterranean with the *Kansas, Langton Hall, Scindia, Glengyle,* and the *Warcypren* will join with O.L. 24 and the *Elmina, City of Bombay, Tenasserim, Harmodius, British Major,* and the *Eurylochus*. They will travel together as much as possible, but their final destinations span the world; Sierra Leone, Capetown, New York, Boston, Philadelphia, and Savannah River. For the protection of both groups, warships from the United States will cover the convoy with their guns. United States ships *Stevens, Amenn,* and *Shaw* will join forces with British ships *Snowdrop, Sir Bevis,* and the gunboat *Kilgobnet* to offer protection. The *Kilgobnet* always draws attention because of her name and her design. Painted in the dazzle camouflage pattern of bold black and white stripes, she seems to have two bows. She is tapered up at bow and stern to confuse the enemy.

Carpathia is once again on her way to Boston as she was on her maiden voyage years ago. The million details of operating a liner at sea in wartime have been checked and rechecked. The normal Particulars of Engagement have been signed and transfers of officer and crew have been completed. Chief Officer George Cove has left the ship. He is destined for the rank of Commodore of the Cunard fleet in his future. New Chief Officer S.W. Lansley from HMS *P15* takes his place. From *Carmania*, J.P. Baird replaces Bert Roberts as First Officer. Returning officers George Broad and George Evans fill out the officer's complement. This trip will be easier for Captain Prothero since three of his four officers on the last voyage were all named George. Chief Engineer William Downie – a survivor of the torpedoing and sinking of *Cameronia* in 1917 - takes his place deep in the ship with the black gang. Stewards confirm menus and provisions for the light load of passengers under the supervision of Chief Steward Ernest Pimbley. Hugh Francis will operate the wireless system on this trip to America. Crews on all the liners will vastly outnumber passengers westward bound. *Carpathia* has only 57 passengers to Boston. Those passengers will be treated if needed by young Dr. W.J Core. *Carpathia*'s hallways are lined with hundreds of empty cabins. The largest ship in the convoy, she will occupy the commanding Commodore position and strive to herd her merchant ship charges safely through the dangerous waters. Ships in convoys are to stay six cables apart. An old measurement related originally to the anchor chain; one cable is about 1/10 of a mile. Once again, she has a job to do.

Alone in her cabin, Elizabeth lovingly hangs her wedding dress. Soft ivory with half sleeves, it is simply decorated with delicate flourishes on the bodice and in horizontal lines near the bottom. Tightly tailored, she will only add a simple single strand of pearls around her neck. This will be her last night apart from her soon-to-be husband. The Captain has told Harold that he will perform the wedding service tomorrow afternoon, weather permitting. He had looked slightly skeptical on being told of the request to have the wedding on the rear boat deck and not in a saloon protected from the wind. Reminded of the significance of that location by the Marconi house, he ruefully agreed. The hours are dragging. One whole night yet to get through of adhering to the proprieties of a fiancé on the nearly empty ship before her marriage. She is impatient and feels vaguely unladylike about it. Dinner with the Captain, Chaplain Harris, and her Harold will be filled with war talk and more war talk. The news by wireless of a huge German offensive said to contain over 50 divisions near Reims, France! In Russia, the Bolsheviks are fighting a gruesome civil war and are rumored to be close to capturing the Czar and his entire family! The Americans have just captured Belleau Wood and the Italians sent the Austro-Hungarians fleeing at the Battle of Piave. The news is all positive for the Allies, but the death toll continues to mount. As does the worldwide scourge of the flu. Tonight though, Elizabeth wants only to think of tomorrow when she will be Mrs. Harold Cottam. Dinner slides by in a blur of the warmth of her Harold next to her and the wonder of finally being together. She tries to listen to the conversation, but it makes no impact on her. Harold's tight embrace and light kiss goodnight fill her with sudden warmth. Tomorrow night – their wedding night – he will not leave her. Before vainly trying to sleep, she guiltily pulls out the delicate lace that she will wear tomorrow night, her wedding night. The war can wait. Nothing can touch them now.

Elizabeth greets the red dawn after a night with very little sleep and waits for *Carpathia* to rouse herself. She knows the hours will drag by this day until the big event this afternoon. *Carpathia* is still quietly sleeping while she makes slow progress westward. She steamed out of Liverpool just after 6:45 British Summer Time yesterday but is barely into her voyage. Her convoy partners have her tightly leashed to the slowest of them. Her engines throb softly and slowly in frustration.

Chaplain 4th Class Webster Henry Fanning Harris sits in his rolling chair inhaling the warm salt air near the Marconi house just after noon. The sea seems peaceful. *Carpathia* is steaming placidly along after leaving Bishop's Rock lighthouse far behind them. This is a favored hunting ground of many German Captains but seems completely peaceful now. Nothing to be seen. He is partially sheltered from the sticky warm wind by the lifeboats on both sides. Stewards had carried him up the steel stairs after breakfast and he has been relaxing and waiting for his important duty. Finally, he hears many footsteps climbing the ladder.

"Where is the Captain?"

"Miss Hadnot. He received an urgent U-Boat warning and doesn't feel that he can leave his bridge presently. He is, after all, in the Commodore position of the convoy so he has extra duties in addition to just the *Carpathia*. He suggested that I might be of assistance unless you have an objection. He has also told me of the reason you wish to marry in this place on this ship. She has indeed not only been the reason you two met but the reason you are alive, my dear. I think it a fine thing that you decided to have the Lord join you as one and start your new life on this ship. Do you have any objections to my assistance?"

"Well…. I suppose not. What do you think my dear?"

"I think it perfectly suited Elizabeth. I have no objections."

"I can assure you, Miss Hadnot, that I can do a first-rate job of it. I have performed many marriage ceremonies. I can also assure you that I make no distinction regarding the differences between Mr. Luther's beliefs and the Anglican faith. I have seen too much in the trenches to let anything stand in the way of God's happiness in marriage. It would be my honor to join you two if you allow it."

"Well, certainly Chaplain Harris. I would be honored. I was just surprised. What a day this will be!"

Out of sight over the horizon, the Norwegian sailing ship *Miefield* is being shelled by U-55. A coal carrier of 1,386 tons, she will be sunk with scuttling charges set by the Germans after her capture. Her crew is set adrift southwest of Fastnet, Ireland.

'I take thee Harold to be my wedded husband, to have and to hold from this day forward, for better for worse, for richer for poorer, in sickness and in health, to love, cherish, and to obey, till death us do part, according to God's holy ordinance; and thereto I give thee my troth.'

Across war-torn Europe and Russia, the savagery continues this day. French and American troops around Reims, France contain the German advance and push back across the bloody ground. In Russia already abdicated Czar Romanov, his wife Alexandra, their five children, and four servants are herded down into a cellar supposedly for a picture to prove they are alive. When they are all lined up, men rush in and shoot the entire group. Those still alive after the shots ceased are stabbed to death. Chaos, disease, and starvation envelope Russia with an estimated final death toll of 15 million people.

'Oh eternal God, creator and preserver of all mankind, giver of all spiritual grace, the author of everlasting life: send thy blessing upon these thy servants, this man and this woman, whom we bless in they name; that as Isaac and Rebecca lived faithfully together, so these persons may surely perform and keep the vow and covenant betwixt them made and may ever remain in perfect love and peace together, and live according to thy laws through Jesus Christ our Lord. Lord, let me add my own personal wish for these two: that they have peace and love and happiness in this horrible time of war. May they find nothing but peace, safety, and love all of their days. Amen.'

U-55 slips quietly along, her decks awash, after setting the crew of the *Miefield* adrift in their boats unharmed but far from shore. Captain Werner charges his batteries on the surface as one of his crewmen paints another small symbol on the conning tower to represent another enemy ship sent to the bottom. This voyage is starting like the last. His previous successful war patrol had begun with the sinking of another small ship just like today; the British *War Grange*. He is well on his way to his coveted Blue Max. He just needs another victim. Perhaps a bigger prize next time.

'Almighty God, who at the beginning did create our first parents, Adam and Eve, and did sanctify and join them together in marriage; pour upon you the riches of his grace, sanctify, and bless you, that you may please him both in body and soul, and live together in holy love unto your lives' end. Amen.'

With only 36 Saloon passengers, Mr. and Mrs. Cottam eat their wedding dinner almost alone. The Captain has sent a message with his compliments regretfully saying he would remain on the bridge all night. The other diners each stop at their table and express their good wishes and then leave the young couple on their own. Chaplain Harris also sends his regrets as he feels unwell after his exertions on this exhausting day. Except for a champagne toast – courtesy of the Captain - the newlyweds dine like everyone else that night: fricassee of tripe, roast beef, boiled potatoes followed by an apple tart, and coffee.

"Harold, this might actually be the same cabin. I do not recall the cabin number, but this looks exactly like when I was on *Carpathia* with my mother after the *Titanic*."

"Mrs. Cottam, it might look the same. Most of the cabins do. This was the best I could arrange what with the conversion of *Carpathia* to a trooper."

"Say that again."

"What?"

"The part with Mrs. Cottam in it."

"Mrs. Cottam, it might look the same. Most of the cabins do."

"Thank you, my love. I heard the part I wanted. I hope you realize that I meant no dissatisfaction or concern with the cabin. This will be perfect, and that horrible night was so long ago. Another and different life. I know I will never be in that same position again. I was so young then and dependent on my Father. Now, Dearest Harold, I will depend on you. And love you. Now please excuse me for just a moment."

Their wedding night begins as she emerges in a cloud of soft lace that whispers as she walks to the bed. After years of letters, visits, wanting for more, the young couple can experience the first touches, discoveries, mistakes, awkwardness, and joys of their first night together. The ship's engines throb gently through the bones of the ship through the night as they lie together in the rucked sheets. Whispered words of love and the future disappear into the darkness of the small cabin before they sleep.

As of July 17, 1918 dawns, the Allies begin their decisive counterattack in France seizing the initiative for good in the European war. U-37, U-60, and U-70 have already struck this day, sending four ships to their graves. Yesterday, ten ships had fallen victim to the German sea hunters on the day of the Cottam wedding. Wilhelm Werner has submerged and begun his hunting at dawn this morning.

Smiling and happy, the newlyweds pay no attention to the news this bright morning. The remnants of their omelets, golden cakes, and scones, litter the plates as they sit and talk and laugh happily in the dining saloon. *Carpathia* is now steaming in what is thought to be safer territory and her escorts have divided when the convoy split into two separate groups around 8:15 this morning. Easily the largest ship in the O.L. 24, *Carpathia* takes a central position in the three lines of ships steaming slowly westward. Harold and Elizabeth linger over coffee. They are in no hurry to go anywhere or do anything besides revel in their new status. The Captain once again sends his compliments. Elizabeth tucks away the small card; the first example of something addressed to Mr. and Mrs. Harold Cottam.

Built by Friedrich Krupp Germaniawerft and commissioned just over two years ago on June 8, 1916, the U-55 is just one of the millions of weapons of war produced by the sprawling Krupp armaments empire. Krupp produces most of the artillery of the Imperial German Army, including its heavy siege guns: the 420 mm Big Bertha, the 1916 Langer Max, and the seven Paris guns. The gun called Batterie Pommern is the largest gun in the world in 1917. In addition, Krupp builds German warships and submarines in Kiel. Krupp's products are always well known for their reliability, efficiency, and lethality. Now, less than 3,000 yards off the port side of the unsuspecting *Carpathia*, Kapitänleutnant Werner makes the final calculations as he lines up his death-dealing torpedoes on the soaring walls filling his periscope. This will be his biggest prize yet. Huge and inviting. A certain bet to guarantee his Blue Max. Two torpedoes are poised impatiently in his bow tubes ready to fire. Just under 20 feet in length and able to close the distance at 35 knots, their 60% TNT/40% Hexanite explosive mixture is very reliable and deadly efficient. He steadies his view through the periscope and makes the final targeting calculations. His quiet commands are echoed by his experienced attack team in U-55. His breathing slows, and he wills his heart to beat quietly and softly and tries to quell the excitement of the hunter who has set the perfect trap and has his prey in his sights. He only betrays his excitement when he calls out the German command so relished by the U-Boat crews.

"TORPEDO LOS!"

The stewards are doing the final clearing of breakfast for the late rising passengers and preparing for the afternoon's activities and meals. The day is bright and warm, with a low running sea. A perfect day to relax on deck. The newlyweds look forward to their first full day as Mr. and Mrs. Cottam filled with promenading and lounging on the deck. And making love below decks.

"HERE SHE COMES!' screams a steward as he points to the sea.

Chapter Ten

DEATH OF A LADY

They are on the central staircase under the bridge when it strikes. They planned to walk the promenade deck together on their first morning as husband and wife. Elizabeth trails her small fingers across the carved woodwork and breathes the damp wood smell this area of the ship gives off on humid mornings – even after all these years. A ship's steward had told her that this was one way that 'the old girl' told them a storm was coming soon. More reliable than any weather report or scan of the sky, the stairway area is the place to know what was to come he said.

Without warning, their world explodes. Just as they step onto the bottom landing, they are thrown across the second-class entrance lobby and tossed like rag dolls onto the long bench opposite the stairway. The ceiling light fixtures shatter showering them with shards of glass.

"Elizabeth, are you all right my love?"

"Yes, love. I think so. What has happened? Are you hurt Harold?"

"No, I am not hurt. We are alright. Do not worry. Let me catch my breath a minute and think. Well, we are right over the boilers and the stokehold so it could be something from one of those. I wouldn't think it was a torpedo since we are the center ship in formation, but I don't really know. Either way, if you are sure you are alright, let us get ourselves out on deck to see what has happened."

The first torpedo penetrates her steel sides between the port bridge and the number four hold. *Carpathia* gives a wounded lurch but continues along for a few seconds. She heaves a big sigh of air and smoke out of the fidley behind the bridge. Extending from deep in her belly, the fidley vents run straight up from her hard-working boilers to the fresh air above her top deck. Only seconds later another rush of air, smoke, and fire shoots out of the fidley as a second explosion rocks the ship. A second torpedo has cut *Carpathia* open deep in her most vital organs. She is badly hurt as the second German torpedo catches her in the vital beating heart of her engine room. Five members of her black gang immediately perish and two are horribly scalded by fire and steam. *Carpathia* tries to stagger on – despite her wounds - but glides to a stop. Her engine room is a wrecked mass of smoke, fire, and mangled steel. Water gushes in through the two holes in her hull. She is starting to sink; down by the head and listing to port. Electricity is out in the now-darkened ship. One of her lifeboats is now nothing but torn fragments of wood hanging from the charred davit. The wireless has been knocked out so she cannot communicate at any distance.

"ALL HANDS TO THE BOAT STATIONS!" Captain Prothero shouts his orders quickly and decisively. The rigorous training he has done will now be put to the test. "Officers Lansley and Baird, you take charge of the deck crew and loading and lowering the boats. No one is to go below for belongings. The Chief Officer, First and Second Officers, and the gunners are to remain on board. Officers Broad and Evans, see to it that all confidential books and documents are weighted and sent overboard. Send up the daylight star rockets. Signalman, signal the other ships of our condition and check with Mr. Francis to see if our wireless is still operating at all. If not, make sure we get an acknowledgment that the signal flag message has been received and our position sent out by another ship. Officers, get a count, and let's get everyone into the boats before that damned U-Boat fires another into our side. Have the doctor report to me the extent of any casualties and have Engineer Downie give me an update on the condition of the engines – as if it weren't obvious. Find Purser Owen and confirm that he is taking care of all accounts and other issues of the type. The old girl is hurt but maybe not done for. She is sinking slowly. Maybe we can get a towline on her if she stays afloat. She has got a good stout heart and won't let us down. I would hate to have to leave her out here."

Harold and Elizabeth make their way up the stairs to the boat deck. Smoke billows up *Carpathia*'s port side from the gaping holes in her side. Memories of the past overwhelm Elizabeth. Down at the bow and a list to one side. It is the *Titanic* all over again! She sees the remains of a lifeboat shredded by the explosion dangling unusable from their davits.

"Oh my God. It is happening again."

"Now Elizabeth. This is not the same. I am here to help. We only have 57 passengers plus the crew to get off. That is many many hundreds of people less than last time. Lots of lifeboat space for everyone. Do not worry. It will work out. I promise you."

"I'll see you in New York. That is what he said. I'll see you in New York."

"What are you saying? We are not going to New York. We are bound for Boston."

"I'll see you in New York. I never saw him again after that. He promised me."

"Who are you talking about? Elizabeth?"

Under orders from the Vice Commodore in *Tenasserim*, the *Elmina, City of Bombay, Hamodius* and the other ships in the convoy push their boilers to the limit and scatter away from *Carpathia* and the attacking U-Boat at full speed. She is left alone – wounded and hunched over in pain. Before steaming away from the wounded liner signal flags acknowledge her cry for a working wireless to send out the call for help. Her deck crew and officers begin to lower multiple lifeboats from her sides for the first time since April 18, 1912, when she had lowered *Titanic's* recovered lifeboats at the pier in New York. Today, eleven lifeboats will be let down the slanting sides of *Carpathia*. With less than 300 total people on board, there will be room for all. There will be no panicked rush of over a thousand people left on board hoping for salvation as in 1912. It is daylight and those lining the rails waiting to load know that friends are heading to their aid. It is just a question of time. The danger of the U-Boat is also near, however, and the stories of atrocities are filling everyone's minds as they wait.

"Elizabeth? We will get through this. This isn't like the *Lusitania* or the *Titanic*. We have plenty of time, very few people to load into the boats, and *Carpathia* won't fail us. She will give us the time we need. She saved your life once and will do so once again."

The RMS *Lusitania* had been struck by a single torpedo fired by U-20 in 1917. She sank in only 18 minutes. Many of her lifeboats couldn't be lowered. Some capsized, some flipped while being loaded spilling the occupants, and then crashed down on them. 1,200 of her 1,900 passengers and crew would not live out the day.

Elizabeth stands clutching the rail with white knuckles and stares unseeing out at the heaving sea. She doesn't even turn to look at her new husband or seem to hear his words of reassurance. She stares at the threatening sea and mumbles indistinctly.

"My Father. That is what he promised me. That he would see me in New York. I never saw him again. Now it is happening again. I will never see my mother again. Never. We will all go into the freezing sea as he did. I didn't see him in New York or anywhere again. I had to sit in that freezing boat with a dead man at my feet and hear my Father drown. I can hear him now. I can hear the screams of all those people in the water splashing and screaming until they got quiet. And died. Like we will now." She stands shivering uncontrollably in the July heat.

On board the wounded liner, the gunners remain scanning the sea at their station while trying to hold their footing on the slanting deck as the stern of the ship rises. Soon the height of the stern above the water makes any gun actions impossible. The classified materials are put in weighted sacks and tossed over the side. The doctor is doing his best to treat two wounded engineers who miraculously manage to find their way topside from the engine room. They are horribly scalded, and Doctor Core soothes them as best he can with applications of oil to their burns. Chaplain Harris ministers to the men before he and his rolling chair are manhandled down into a lifeboat. The angle of the deck sharply increases. Her stern rises further out of the water as her bow dips below the surface. She is sinking faster now. Few lifeboats remain. One is somehow lowered by two inexperienced cooks and one officer containing the scalded engineers and the doctor. The last lifeboat is held for Captain Prothero, the quartermasters, and the gunners. The five dead of the black gang will remain deep within the ship forever.

<u>*Carpathia*</u> <u>Killed in Action July 17, 1918</u>

Charles Hughes, 32 yrs, Fireman

James Murphy, 46 yrs, Fireman

Frank O'Neill, 22 yrs, Trimmer

Edward Hamilton, 19 yrs, Trimmer

Reginald Peters, 26 yrs, Trimmer

"Elizabeth, listen to me. Look at me! We will get into this lifeboat right in front of us. We will both get into the boat. I will be with you. No one will be left on board. There is plenty of room, see? It is not that midnight darkness you had before. It is not freezing cold either. It is plain daylight, and I am here to make sure nothing happens to you. Ever. These damnable U-Boats don't usually lay about for long. They know we have sloops and other warships that come to our aid. They know to get out of the area to save their skins. The signalman got an acknowledgment that our flag messages were received, and a wireless signal was sent calling for help. The Marconi man confirmed that that signal was received as well. We may have to float a bit – but certainly, this will not be anything like you did last time. Come now my love, it is time to board. You will be all right my love."

"Come along Mrs. Cottam. It is time to leave. I will help you and your husband to safety. All will be well." The tall form of Captain Prothero gently approaches Elizabeth as she stands frozen at the ship's rail. More than a head taller than her at 5'10", his bulk provides a reassuring presence.

"Father?"

"No, Mrs. Cottam. It is Captain Prothero. Let's get you to safety now. We need to move right along." The Captain pries her white-knuckled hands from the rail and sweeps her up in his arms. Motioning to Harold to get into the lifeboat, he puts the new bride into her husband's arms in the boat before she realizes what is happening. The ropes creak and the pulleys rattle as the boat is lowered away. The Captain is long gone before Harold can even thank him. There is still much to be done on his suffering ship, and one more lifeboat to be launched.

Carpathia groans again in pain as the sound of collapsing steel deep within her rings out. She seems desperate to avoid joining her Cunard sisters already at the bottom. The *Andania* was sunk by U-46, *Aurania* sunk by U-67, and *Ausonia* –who had survived a damaging torpedo strike by Werner in U-55 in 1917 - succumbed to U-62 in May of 1918. By now all living souls have left the old girl. No more immigrants will travel to the new world in her. No more soldiers will be complaining about the food in her on the way to war-torn Europe. She will not make any more high-speed dashes through an iceberg-strewn sea to the rescue. The plaque commemorating her heroics on that cold night in April 1912 is now underwater. Her great and anonymous days are now behind her. She will not celebrate the end of the War to end all Wars in a few scant months. Her lifeboats are grouped on the sea, and some of the overcrowded boats are engaged in the tricky business of transferring passengers from one boat to another on the open sea. They float alone in silence. About an hour later their tense solitude is broken when a periscope appears suddenly followed by the rest of the U-Boat breaking the surface and slowly approaching.

There it is! Right in front of him. The biggest target of his entire career. This will certainly do it. The Pour le Mérite – Das Blauer Max – The Blue Max will soon be placed around his neck. He will be required to wear it at all times when in uniform. It can only be given by Prussian royalty. As he squints through the periscope, Kapitänleutnant Werner smiles to himself at the irony of the French name for a German decoration. So typical that when the Blue Max was first conceived, French was the preferred language at the German royal court. How intertwined and confused European history is. But now there is no doubt of what will win Werner the medal. One sinking of over 13,000 tons right in the English backyard. He will join other Germans like Baron von

Richtofen, Ernst Udet, Erwin Rommel, Alfred von Tirpitz, and Otto von Bismark in wearing the blue and gold recognition of bravery and devotion to duty. No room for mistakes now. He will approach within ¼ mile of the listing steamer. It is taking too long for the ship to sink. He will shoot one more torpedo at this wounded target to make sure and attempt to retrieve her ensign as proof. If he cannot collect her flag, then he will decide what to do about the people in the lifeboats. One of them would be proof as well.

"TORPEDO LOS!'

The torpedo smashes into the *Carpathia* almost under her once-famous Marconi house. This is a fatal blow. She can fight no more. A huge explosion hides her from the sight of both attacker and victims already in the water. She begins her fatal plunge bow first. The red Cunard ensign is seen fluttering from her stern as it rises above the smoke. Nearly two and one-half hours after the first impact – almost exactly the same life span as the *Titanic* after her collision – *Carpathia* breathes her last and sinks from sight. As she sinks to her resting place a thundering explosion of at least one of her boilers bursting further shatters her engine room. She is past feeling. Settling in the deep darkness over 500 feet below the surface, she ends her journeys.

U-55 slowly turns towards the floating lifeboats. The crewmen on her rolling deck can be clearly seen as they swivel the 88 mm deck gun menacingly towards the helpless *Carpathia* survivors. The tall, peaked cap of the Captain is visible, along with another officer on the conning tower with a camera. He is seen taking pictures of the sinking liner. Those in the small boats can only await their fate. Will the German Captain use his deck gun to blow the small boats to bits as others have done? Will he ram the boats sending them to the bottom? Will he take Captain Prothero back to Germany as a prize? As it approaches each detail of the killing machine can be seen. It is not one of the latest U-Boats but still deadly effective at killing.

Outstretched arms of the lookouts can be seen on top of the U-Boat. A matching chorus of arms from the floating lifeboats mimics the pose moments later. A smudge of dark smoke on the horizon has been spotted. Very faintly a distant pounding of gunfire can be heard. Magically all life on the U-Boat vanishes and its menacing shape slides silently beneath the waves. Coming flat out at her maximum speed of 17 knots, the HMS *Snowdrop* charges to the hunt with all flags flying. Launched in 1915, *Snowdrop* was one of the convoy protection and mine sweeping ships built under the Emergency War Program by Britain. Half the size and beam of *Carpathia*, they aren't built for comfort, but to protect the water lifeline of the British Empire and sting her enemies. These small, quick warships belie their peaceful names and demonstrate the English love of flowers and gardens – even in wartime. HMS *Azalea, Begonia, Carnation, Peony,* and *Zinnia* are some of these small tough fighting ships. *Snowdrop*'s 2 - Mark IX guns are firing as fast as their operators can operate them. While a bit awkward to handle for rapid-fire, the guns have a range of 13,000 yards and the 31-pound shells are starting to reach the last position of U-55. The cheers of the survivors in the boats cause Elizabeth to look up for the first time.

"Look Elizabeth! Look! We will be safe now! Help is here! I think he will pass us by and hunt the U-Boat, but we will be safe and sound now. It is just a matter of time. We need to be patient for just a bit longer." For the first time since the realization the *Carpathia* was under attack, Elizabeth's eyes swim into focus and she gives Harold a weak smile.

Snowdrop surges past the waiting boats and keeps to the attack. Thick black smoke is pouring out of *Snowdrop*'s funnels as her coal-fired boilers push her to top speed. Shells join the *Carpathia* on the bottom of the sea as the sloop hunts her prey. As she charges past the floating lifeboats signal flags waggle from her bridge assuring the boats that she will return. But for now, she has a job to do. As soon as she clears the lifeboats, she begins to pummel the sea with her Mark III depth charges. With a kill radius of only 14 feet, *Snowdrop* needs to be right on top of the U-Boat to get a kill when the 300 pounds of Amatol explodes. She lays a pattern for her depth charges and then dashes off to another spot and roils that part of the sea. Merchant seamen and passengers alike in the boats are transfixed by the action as *Snowdrop* does her work. Even Elizabeth seems released from her spell and watches as the sloop works in ever-widening circles away from the floating survivors of *Carpathia*. Soon the warship is lost to sight. Only the distant sounds of explosions can be heard.

After a total of nearly three hours in the boats, *Snowdrop* returns. Disappointed and exhausted from their futile chase, her sailors now set about picking up the survivors from the Cunard liner. A disembodied voice from her bridge instructs Captain Prothero to have his boats approach the sloop one at a time. Once again, the delicate dance is performed to get all up the sides of a rescue ship safely. The scalded and oil-covered seamen are hauled aboard on stretchers and immediately taken below with the two ships' doctors. Unlike *Carpathia*'s rescue of the *Titanic* survivors, this time there is no room on board to save her lifeboats. They are abandoned and float sadly away from the warship. The last traces of *Carpathia* scatter and float empty on the Atlantic.

HMS *Snowdrop* had been built in Dunbarton, Scotland for war and not for comfort. There are no 'comfortable and friendly' features and cabins on the small sloop. She is crewed by 79 officers and men. Every inch of her was filled with either men or equipment for her tasks. No dining saloons or deluxe cabins. No promenade deck, no public lavatories. Now she takes on 276 survivors of the sinking. She will be challenged as never before to accommodate all the people. Just keeping them all safe and on board the ship until arriving in Queenstown will be a miracle with the weather coming in tonight. The oldest and frailest of the women take the officers' cabins. The rest need to find a few feet for themselves on deck. The officers and men of *Carpathia* will stand and watch over their passengers from both a sense of duty and a lack of space. Elizabeth refuses any attempt to put her in a cabin away from Harold. The young couple claims a tiny spot near the front mast and sits huddled under a blanket given to them by a seaman with a barbarous cockney accent. They smile and nod their thanks without understanding anything he has said to them.

"I'm so sorry Harold. I don't know what came over me. I am usually the brave one. I just…It was so much like…All I could see was…I could hear his voice again…I'm sorry Harold."

Pulling the shared blanket closer around them, Harold makes it more private. "It is all right my love. I do understand. You don't always have to be the brave one. We can share those duties from now on. You were very brave – so brave you took my breath away in 1912 - and you have continued to be brave for both you and your mother all these years. You have gone through hell at sea twice now. You are entitled to not be perfect at all times and I think a torpedo attack is an excuse enough for anyone."

"But, darling, you have always said I was perfect. At least up till now."

"Ah, it is good to see you smile again. You have always been perfect to me."

"Well done Mr. Cottam. Very good recovery there. Now, since it looks like we will be sitting here throughout the night, we will have plenty of time to discuss our future. I must tell you my sweet Harold that I will not get on another ship. Never again. I just cannot. I will miss my mother and family in America very much, but can you work in England so we can just stay there when we land?"

"Well, Elizabeth that is certainly not what we planned. I will have to think a moment. I am sure I can get wireless work, but probably not as large of a selection of ships as I would have in New York."

"Harold, I don't want you working on ships anymore darling."

"What?"

"Well I have been thinking on this for some time; even before today. I could not stand to lose you. I don't want to end up like my mother in an attic somewhere. Plus, if you were to be in a shore berth, we could be together and start our family. Even if you are safe but still gone for months at a time, it will be very hard. And I don't want you on any more ships."

"Well…. I know we spoke of this for the future. I just had not considered it as happening right away. Let's get situated when we are on dry land again and decide our next move."

The decision is made for them later that same night. A shore job it will be. No more discussion is needed. Just before midnight, a lashing gale rocks the small ship. Waves crash over the bow and attempt to sweep everything and everyone off the decks. The passengers on deck are roped to the fittings and guns on deck. They spend a fearful eternity clutching anything within reach to keep from being washed overboard in the huge swells. Lightning cracks across the wide ocean sky and the thunder makes the small ship shake. Somehow, between bolts of white-hot lightning, the wireless receives an order. *Snowdrop* will not go to Queenstown, Ireland but is ordered to Liverpool directly. There the shaken passengers of *Carpathia* that survived both a torpedo attack and this hellish night of storms will disembark and make their plans. Some will find another ship to risk another war-time trip to

America. Some will take the extra month's pay Cunard offers and wait for another ship to employ them since their last berth is at the bottom of the Atlantic. And some like the Cottam newlyweds will decide not to go back to America but build a new life ashore in England; never again to venture down to the sea in ships.

When Arthur Rostron – the hero of the *Titanic* – hears of *Carpathia*'s fate, his words are simple. 'It was a sorry end to a fine ship, yet it is fitting. She had done her bit both in peace and war, and she lies in her natural element, resting her long rest on a bed of sand.'

AFTERWORD

RMS Carpathia

Keel laid	9/10/01	Length	558'
Launched	8/6/02	Beam	64'
M. Voyage	5/5/03	1st Captain	James Barr
Sunk	7/17/18	Last Captain	Wm. Prothero
Wreck found	2000	Passenger Cap.	2,550

Carpathia, in her short history, carried tens of thousands of immigrants to America. While exact numbers are very difficult to find, if you give her the same basic occupancy of the non-war years of 1908-1913, 80,000-100,000 total passengers could have been carried safely on her voyages during her life. Tens of thousands of Allied troops made the journey safely to Europe during WW1. At least three of the seven Cunard Commodores who earned knighthood served on *Carpathia*. The last living American veteran of WW1 had been carried to Europe on her. Considering the thousands of new families to the USA and their descendants, the American and Canadian troops being transported to Europe, the training and service of her officers that went on to serve so ably on future ships, and over seven hundred saved from the *Titanic* and their descendants; the impact of the RMS *Carpathia* is incalculable.

The wreck of the *Carpathia* was first tentatively located in 1999 and confirmed in 2000. She is sitting upright on the bottom 514 feet below the surface 120 miles south of Fastnet, Ireland. There are large tears in her side from torpedo strikes and possible boiler explosions. She is covered in marine growth and lost fishing nets. Her superstructure has collapsed as well as her masts and funnel. She is surrounded by various debris including both her own ammunition and shells fired by HMS *Snowdrop* in 1918. There is no visible trace of her Marconi house on the aft boat deck.

Harold Cottam

Harold Thomas Cottam is born 1/27/1891 in Southwell, Nottinghamshire, England. He completes the Marconi School program at the age of 17, the youngest to graduate that school. He works in wireless postings on shore and at sea, including amongst others, the RMS *Empress of Ireland*, the SS *Medic*, and a telegraphist at the British post office on land. He testifies in both the American and British *Titanic* enquiries. He marries Elsie Shepperson in 1922 and takes a quiet sales job at the Mini Max Fire Extinguisher Company. He and Elsie have four children. He is very reticent about talking about his *Titanic* experience and stung personally with the criticism of accepting money for his *New York Times* interview in 1912. He dies 5/30/1984.

Arthur Rostron

Arthur Henry Rostron is born 5/14/1869 in Bolton, Lancashire, England. He always dreams of going to sea and does so at age 13. He serves both Cunard and the Royal Naval Reserve until he retires to Southampton in May of 1931. Sir Arthur Rostron is feted around the globe for his actions in the *Titanic* rescue, including receiving the highest civilian medal possible from the United States, the Congressional Gold Medal.

He commands 25 different ships during his career and retires as a Commodore of the Fleet for Cunard. The 'Hero of the *Titanic*' dies 11/4/1940.

James Bisset

James Gordon Bisset is born on 7/18/1883 in Liverpool, England. Eager to go to sea, he stows away on a ship leaving Liverpool at the age of 14 but is found and returned. The following year he officially begins his career at sea and eventually serves on four different ships with Arthur Rostron. He has larger and larger commands culminating in the commands of both *Queen Mary* and *Queen Elizabeth*. He retires as Commodore of the Fleet and moves to Sydney, Australia. He dies on 3/28/1967.

Wilhelm Werner

Wilhelm Werner is born 6/6/1888 in Apolda, Germany. He commands three different U-Boats during World War 1. He is accused of multiple war crimes after the war involving attacking marked hospital ships and also two incidents of bringing survivors of a sinking on his deck and then submerging underneath them leaving them to drown. He escapes to Brazil and is never tried. Coming back to Germany, he becomes a National Socialist member of the Reichstag and a Brigadeführer in the SS during WW2. He dies 5/14/1945.

Guglielmo Marconi

Guglielmo Marconi is born 4/25/1874 in Balogna, Italy. He marries the granddaughter of the founder of the Irish Jameson Whiskey operation. He moves to England when they show interest in his wireless experiments. Widely praised for his system's assistance in the *Titanic* sinking, he continues to expand his business and knowledge of wireless systems. He will be known as the father of radio. He returns to Italy during WW1 and accomplishes the unlikely feat of being a senator in the Italian Senate, and both a commissioned Naval and Army officer. He is part of the Italian mission to the United States both in 1917 and 1919. He dies 7/20/1937 in Rome.

List of ships and final disposition

RMS Carpathia	Sunk by torpedo 7/17/18
RMS Titanic	Sunk by collision with iceberg 4/15/12
U-55	Sold to Japan after WW1 dismantled 1921
SS Californian	Sunk 11/9/15 by U-35
CS Mackay-Bennett	Scrapped in 1963
RMS Olympic	Retired from service 1935
RMS Britannic	Sunk by collision with mine 11/21/16
SS Virginian	Retired from service 1954
SS Mount Temple	Scuttled by Germans after capture 12/6/16
SS Frankfurt	Scrapped in Japan 1931
SS Baltic	Scrapped in Japan 1933
HMS Snowdrop	Sold for breakup 1/15/23
USS DeKalb	Scrapped 1934
USS Lea	Scrapped 1945

Sources List

Behe, George. *Voices of the Carpathia: Rescuing the Titanic*, The History Press, 2015

Bisset, Sir James. *Tramps and Ladies, My Early Years in Steamers*, London, 1959

Bosworth, Katherine and Hughes, Michael. *Titanic calling – Wireless Communications During the Great Disaster*, Bodleian Library, University of Oxford, 2012

Britten, Sir Edgar. *A Million Ocean Miles*, Hutchinson & Co., 1989

Clements, Eric. *Captain of the Carpathia: The Seafaring Life of Titanic Hero Sir Arthur Henry Rostron*, Conway – Bloomsbury Publishing, 2016.

McNamara, M.J. *Personal diary of service WW1*, Bill Baird, 2002

Pickenpaugh, Roger. *Carpathia – A Biography of the Titanic's Rescue Ship*, Otter Bay Books 2011

Rostron, Sir Arthur. *The Loss of the Titanic*, Titanic Signals Archive, 1991

Rostron, Sir Arthur. *Home from the Sea: Autobiography of Captain Rostron of the Carpathia*, MacMillian Company, 1931

Swavely, Clarence. *One Hundred Years in the Andhra Country – History of the India Mission of the ULCA 1842-1942*

Various Newspaper archives including *New York Times, Liverpool Daily Post, New York Herald*

Wilson, Andrew. *Shadow of the Titanic: The Extraordinary Stories of Those Who Survived*, Atria books, 2011.

Printed in Great Britain
by Amazon